"He created the old
man with his loosely
jointed, hanging
arms, and made
him walk with
heavy, dragging
step, the worn-out
walk of old men.
He gave him an
expression of
weariness that runs
over his face and
down into his beard.
He created the man
who carried the key. In
him there is still life
enough for many years to
come, but all of it is
compressed into this
sudden final hour. His lips
are tightly clamped
together, his hands bite into
the key. He has set fire to
his strength, and it is
consumed within him, in
his stubborn defiance. He
created the man who
buries his drooping head
in his hands, as if to
collect himself, to be alone
for just one more
moment. He created the
two brothers, one of
whom looks back, while
the other lowers his head
in a gesture of
determination and
submission, as if he were
already offering it to the
executioner.

"And he created the enigmatic gesture of the man who 'is just passing through life' [Gustave Geffroy]. He is already on his way, but he turns back once more, not towards the city, not towards those who are in tears, not towards his companions. He turns back towards himself. He raises his right arm; it bends, wavers; his hand opens in the air and releases something, just as one might give a bird its freedom.

"This gesture symbolizes the release of all uncertainty, of happiness yet to come, of sorrow that will now wait in vain, of men, wherever they might live, whom he might have met some day, of all the possibilities of tomorrow and the day after that, and also of death, which he had always imagined to be very far away, quiet and gentle, and only at the end of a long, a very long time. Erected on its own in a shady old garden, this figure would be a fitting monument for all those who have died before their time.

And this is how Rodin breathed life into each one of these men, through the final gesture of their lives."

Rainer Maria Rilke *Rodin*, 1902

(Unless otherwise stated, all Rilke quotations are from *Rodin*, 1902).

CONTENTS

RODIN
THE HANDS OF GENIUS
Hélène Pinet

THAMES AND HUDSON

"Michelangelo and Raphael are great names, but we can match them ... you said. That was when we lived in another world, full of illusions; we could already see the clouds parting to let crowns of glory drop upon our heads. Then, pausing, you would yearn to penetrate the shadows and read what fate had in store for you at the age of twenty."

CHAPTER ONE
"YOU WERE BORN FOR ART"

Léon Fourquet, a sculptor friend of Rodin, was nostalgically recalling the time when, at the age of sixteen, they had great expectations of life, when it seemed nothing could stand in their way, neither poverty, nor discouragement, nor jealousy. Right: The young Rodin, c. 1862. Left: *Four o'clock at the Salon* by François Biard (1798–1882).

François-Auguste-René, the second child of the Rodin family, was born on 12 November 1840 in the Rue de l'Arbalète in Paris. Two years earlier his father's second marriage, to Marie Cheffer, had resulted in the birth of a daughter: Maria. Jean-Baptiste Rodin, who was originally from Yvetot in Normandy, came from a family of cotton merchants. Like many others, encouraged by the Industrial Revolution, he had left the provinces in the 1820s to look for work in Paris. There he obtained a post as a junior office clerk at the Préfecture de Police; Auguste Rodin always drew a discreet veil over his father's profession.

A modest, quiet family life, a 'dark and uncertain' childhood

On Sundays, after mass at the church of Saint-Médard,

Jean-Baptiste Rodin, Rodin's father (above), spent a few months as a lay brother in a religious community before obtaining a post at the Préfecture de Police in Paris, where he remained until his retirement as a local police inspector in 1861. Left: The confirmation of his appointment as office clerk, dated 1827. The police were a vitally important instrument for the various political regimes, from the Restoration through to the Second Empire, and with a salary of 1800 francs a month, Rodin's father was well able to provide for his family. He was aged thirty-eight on the birth of his son, Auguste, and his wife was thirty-four.

the family would go for a walk in the Jardin des Plantes or the countryside around Paris, in the Bois de Meudon. Sometimes Auguste's aunt, Thérèse Cheffer, would join them with her three sons. The two families saw a great deal of each other, and Rodin later remained close to his cousins Auguste, Emile and Henri.

Marie Cheffer, originally from Gorze, in the Moselle region, had moved to Paris with two of her sisters. In 1836, at the age of twenty-nine, she married Jean-Baptiste Rodin. The couple were very religious, and their children's education was characterized by the 'solid and manly virtues of the common people', tempered by the 'gracious courtesy' of the 18th century. On Rodin's mother's side there is evidence of a penchant for the artistic life; his three Cheffer cousins became, respectively, an engraver, a draughtsman and a typographer; Henri, who ran a small printing works, engraved and printed Rodin's visiting cards. The Rodin family moved frequently, but always within the suburbs of Saint-Marcel and Saint-Jacques, where 'there was plenty of scope for the modern Parisian improvements': Rue de l'Arbalète, Rue des Fossés-Saint-Jacques, Rue des Bourguignons, Rue du Faubourg-Saint-Jacques. The Paris of Rodin's early childhood, with its maze of narrow alleyways, had scarcely changed since 1789.

Though not very outgoing, Auguste was a typical young boy; he provided his own entertainment with whatever came to hand, burying himself in a world of daydreams. 'When I was very young, as long ago as I can remember, I used to draw. At a grocer's where my mother did her shopping, they used to wrap their prunes in paper cones made from the pages of illustrated magazines, and even from engravings. I used to copy them. They were my first models.' Although this may be one of the sculptor's real memories, it could also be an anecdote invented to satisfy his biographers, who were keen to detect signs of early promise.

The young Rodin, who was shy and handicapped by being very short-sighted, had little to show for his time at the Val-de-Grâce primary school, where, like most Parisian children, he was educated by the brothers of the

Ecoles Chrétiennes. He later admitted that he remembered nothing from these years. In an attempt to remedy the situation, Auguste's father sent him to the boys' boarding school run by his uncle Hippolyte in Beauvais. But he failed to progress with his studies there either, and when his uncle decided to send him back to Paris, Auguste still had difficulty with reading and writing, and barely knew how to count. He was by now fourteen, 'the age at which all young boys should start to learn a trade'.

H orace Lecoq de Boisbaudran (left) trained a whole generation of painters and sculptors. 'The true teacher', he believed, 'will never offer himself as an example to his pupils, because the more self-effacing he is, the more he can encourage them to develop their own personalities.' The sculptor Jean-Baptiste Carpeaux also corrected Rodin's studies (below) from time to time; Rodin remembered the 'instinctive admiration' the students felt for him, sensing they were in the presence of a 'great man'.

Auguste convinces his father of his artistic vocation and enrols at the Ecole Impériale

Auguste still had no clear idea about his future. He spent much of his time in the Bibliothèque Sainte-Geneviève, where he happened one day to look at some books of engravings after Michelangelo; they came as a revelation to him, and he decided to devote himself to drawing. Jean-Baptiste Rodin did not consider this a suitable career for his son; he had cherished ambitions more in keeping with their social standing. But Auguste stubbornly refused to abandon the idea, and eventually his father allowed himself to be persuaded by his wife and daughter. In 1854 Auguste began to attend the Ecole Impériale de Dessin, which was commonly known as the Petite Ecole to distinguish it from the more prestigious Ecole des Beaux-Arts.

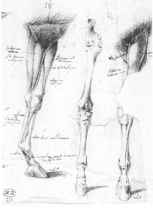

In 1877 this non-feepaying school, first established by Louis XV in 1765, was to become the Ecole Nationale des Arts Décoratifs. Although originally dedicated to the teaching of drawing, it mainly trained artist-craftsmen: cabinetmakers, engravers, locksmiths and metalworkers. Thanks to its director Hilaire Belloc and the teaching of Horace Lecoq de Boisbaudran, however, it acquired a certain prestige in artistic circles. Lecoq de Boisbaudran encouraged his pupils to work from memory, in order to develop their powers of observation and to sharpen their grasp of the overall form and character of a subject. He also urged his pupils to work directly from nature, an idea that was not adopted at the Beaux-Arts until much later. In this way Rodin learned that natural light brings out form to best advantage; he was even to maintain that 'sculpture is a *plein-air* art'.

Rodin was now meeting young people of roughly his own age, who shared the same interests and ambitions. Some of his contemporaries were also to become famous: the painters Henri Fantin-Latour, who had just been admitted to the Ecole des Beaux-Arts, and Alphonse Legros. The sculptor Jules Dalou, who had started two years earlier, became, together with Léon Fourquet, one of Rodin's closest friends.

Rodin spent his time copying antique art (above) and executing the traditional academic studies. Later, under the tuition of Antoine-Louis Barye, he studied animal anatomy (opposite, below left). Below: Rodin's museum pass.

Paris becomes a vast study room for a young man hungry for knowledge

His contact with these companions quickly brought home to Rodin the extent of his ignorance in artistic matters. Eager to fill the gaps in his

knowledge, he attended everything the French capital had to offer in the way of free drawing classes, museums and libraries.

His days were very busy. Before going to the Petite Ecole, he would practise painting at the studio of Pierre Lauset, a painter friend of the family. Then from 8 to 12 am he attended drawing classes in the rotunda of the Ecole Impériale. The training provided there consisted essentially in copying works by the old masters; unlike the Ecole des Beaux-Arts, there were no live models. Teachers were not present all the time, but came on regular days to correct their pupils' work.

Rodin would spend the afternoon in the Louvre,

The Ecole des Beaux-Arts, which was dependent on the Institut, was hostile to any new trends. The admission procedure involved several stages. A competition every six months determined where the student, providing he was accepted, would sit during drawing classes. If he was poorly placed, he could find himself drawing the model's

copying antique sculptures, or in the Bibliothèque Impériale, consulting reference works. He would then attend drawing classes held by Hippolyte Lucas at the Gobelins Tapestry Workshop. Here sessions of work from a live model alternated with the drawing of plaster casts. And in the evening Rodin would draw from memory everything he had seen during the day.

Artistic skill was not enough; Rodin wanted to fill the intellectual and literary gaps that had resulted from his somewhat haphazard education. Encouraged by his friends, he began to read – Homer and Virgil, Victor

back for the entire term. Students had to compete for re-admission at each session, their place in the class being allotted on the basis of their new results. Only by winning a medal in the competition could they secure a permanent place. Above: *The Painting Jury* by Henri Gervex (1852–1929).

Hugo, the great poets Alfred de Musset and Alphonse de Lamartine and the historian Jules Michelet.

'For the first time I saw clay, and I felt as if I were ascending into heaven'

As the first year of study was devoted entirely to drawing, Rodin still knew nothing of sculpture. He discovered it quite by chance when he happened one day to push open the door to the modelling room; he realized at once where his true vocation lay.

For Rodin, as for the majority of 19th-century sculptors, sculpture was synonymous with modelling. His dexterity, the speed with which he worked the clay – in short, his immediate mastery of the technique and the pleasure he derived from it, convinced him that he had found his niche: 'I made separate pieces, arms, heads, feet; then tackled a whole figure. I grasped the whole thing immediately, and with as much ease as I would today. I was in raptures.'

In 1857 Rodin was awarded two first prizes for drawing after the antique. At the age of seventeen, with the encouragement of his teachers, he naturally began to think of applying for the Ecole des Beaux-Arts.

His father was unsure whether to encourage his son's ambitions, so he asked the advice of the sculptor Hippolyte Maindron, an unrivalled master and current darling of the Salons. Having examined the drawings and plaster casts that Auguste brought to his studio in a handcart – they included a bust of Jean-Baptiste

This self-portrait must have been drawn before 1859, the year in which Rodin fell through a shop window. The accident left him with a large scar, which he disguised by growing a beard. Judith Cladel, the sculptor's biographer, writes: 'What unconscious self-confidence we find in the features of this shy young man! A beardless, almost childish face, a straight nose, a mouth tight shut, concealing his secret but unswerving determination, and, above all, the converging arch of his eyebrows, a bow tense with a desire that would never be diminished.' The same air of determination characterizes the bust he modelled of his father, also in 1859 (left), which has all the dignity of a Roman senator.

Rodin, considered Rodin's first independent work – he confirmed that the young man had talent. Strengthened in his resolve by this expert opinion, Rodin tackled the entrance examination for the Beaux-Arts with enormous confidence.

Statue-mania ruled triumphant as Paris underwent drastic reconstruction. Above: The creation of the Rue de Rennes.

Rodin is rejected by the Ecole des Beaux-Arts

Three times Rodin applied for a place and was turned down. His friends, who were astonished by his skilfully modelled works, could not fathom the reason for these rebuffs. But Rodin was steeped in the 18th-century spirit of the Petite Ecole, and was therefore completely out of step with the Neo-classical style of Jacques-Louis David that prevailed at the Ecole des Beaux-Arts.

A sculptor whose work was not in harmony with conventional taste could not expect to be awarded any commissions, and to survive for a moment without commissions was quite unthinkable. Sculpture was an expensive business; there was the cost of the studio (which was never large enough), the materials (clay, plaster, blocks of marble), the bronze-casting and patination, carried out by specialists, not to mention the models and assistants.

Rodin abandons his studies to become an architectural sculptor

In 1861 Jean-Baptiste Rodin retired on a small pension, and Auguste was called upon to make a contribution to the family finances. His sister Maria had been working for some years in a shop selling devotional knick-knacks.

Since 1853 Paris had been undergoing a brutal transformation initiated by Napoleon III and the planner Baron Haussmann, who was effectively minister for the capital until 1870. The improvements to the city involved the erection of numerous statues, and several workshops sprang up to supply the need for decorative stone ornaments. 'Everywhere sculpture

Although Rodin refused to let himself be demoralized by his rejection by the Beaux-Arts, he did suffer occasional bouts of gloom during this period. In a letter headed 'On the subject of work' (below left), Jean-Baptiste Rodin lectured his son: 'Whoever really wants something can get it, and will achieve his goal. I am afraid you're being a bit of a wet, because, it seems to me, you are allowing yourself to be discouraged.' Rodin's fellow student Léon Fourquet (standing next to him in the photograph opposite, above left) gave him a gentle talking to: 'It is not talent you lack – as so many others do – but the energy necessary to bring it to fruition.' He predicted: 'You were born for art, and I was born to carve in marble the ideas that germinated in your mind.' Rodin later realized that he had been extremely fortunate to avoid the pressures and constraints of the Beaux-Arts.

accompanied the vast architectural
programmes, statues began to people
the courtyards, squares and crossroads
newly laid out in the rapidly growing
cities, decorating most of the renovated
public buildings and giving form to
the cult of great men.'

There now began for Rodin
several long, hard years of drifting

from one workshop to another in search of work. His former fellow students at the Petite Ecole, who were all in the same situation, tried their hand at anything they could find: Legros worked as an interior decorator, Dalou modelled animals for a taxidermist, and Fourquet left Paris for Marseilles, where, on the site of the Palais de Longchamp, he worked as a stonemason.

Rodin, meanwhile, was leading a double life: by day he worked for others, by night he made models for his own satisfaction. His first subjects were his family.

A family tragedy interrupts this peaceful working life

After a disappointment in love, Rodin's sister Maria entered the convent of the Holy Infant Jesus as a novice. But she had lost the will to live and died in 1862, a few weeks before pronouncing her vows. Rodin, buried in grief, could imagine no other path than that chosen by his sister. He joined the Fathers of the Holy Sacrament, under the name of Brother Augustin. The community's tolerant and perceptive prior, Father Pierre-Julien Eymard, realizing that the monastic life was not the young man's true vocation, encouraged Rodin to draw and to model, sensing that this was the way to revive his desire to lead an active life. He was proved right, and Rodin soon returned to secular life. He did not go back to live with his parents. Thus, for the first time, he found himself completely independent.

Auguste and Maria (far left, photographed *c.* 1859) were very fond of each other. She was Rodin's confidante, the friend who had faith in his vocation as an artist and defended him against their parents. A firm believer, she offered him a great deal of advice concerning his filial and religious duties.

Father Eymard, founder of the Order of the Holy Sacrament, allowed his new 'recruit' to work in a shed in the community's garden. Like many of the people whose busts were later modelled by Rodin, the priest, who was eventually beatified, did not appreciate the way the sculptor had represented his appearance; he felt that the locks of hair curling over his forehead looked like devil's horns.

" The necessity of making a living forced me to learn every aspect of my profession. I finished bronzes, rough-hewed marble and stone, finished ornaments and jewelry at a silversmith's. I am sorry I wasted so much time, because all the dissipated efforts of those years could have been directed towards producing a fine body of work. Still, it stood me in good stead."

CHAPTER 2

"ALL THE HARDSHIPS OF POVERTY"

"I worked a great deal for other people. Those who, like me, were poor, and had no help from the state, no allowance."

Rodin

Rodin in 1864 (opposite). *Vase des Titans* by Carrier-Belleuse, executed by Rodin (right).

1864 is a year of great changes: Rodin's first studio

'Ah! I will never forget my first studio; I spent some hard times there. As I couldn't afford anything better, I rented a stable in the Rue Lebrun, near the Gobelins, for 120 francs a year. It seemed sufficiently well lit, and there was enough space for me to step back and compare my clay model with the original – a fundamental principle to which I have always adhered. The badly fitting windows and warped wooden door allowed cold air to filter through from every direction, while the roof slates, worn by time or displaced by the wind, created a permanent draught. It was icy cold, and it felt permanently damp, thanks to a well sunk in one corner, which was close to overflowing. Even now I wonder how I stood it.'

The meeting with Rose Beuret

In 1864, while working on the caryatids for the façade of the Théâtre des Gobelins, Rodin met Rose, a twenty-year-old seamstress who worked nearby. Fearing, perhaps, the reaction, Rodin did not introduce her to his family until after the birth of their son, on 18 January 1866. Although the child was given his Christian name, Auguste, Rodin did not legally acknowledge paternity, and he did not marry Rose until two weeks before her death in 1917, by which time she had been his devoted companion for fifty-three years.

The young couple found it very hard to make ends meet. Rose worked at home and posed for Rodin. She was the model for a large *Bacchante*, which Rodin worked on for over two years. When it was smashed during a move to a new studio, Rodin was heartbroken.

An opening at the Carrier-Belleuse studio

By working for Albert-Ernest Carrier-Belleuse, one of the most fashionable and prolific sculptors of the Second

"My model didn't have the grace of city women, but she had all the physical vigour and firm flesh of a farmer's daughter, combined with that lively, frank, determined masculine air that increases the beauty of a woman's body.... Added to that, to make this precise description complete, she was always ready to devote herself to me; which is what she did throughout her life." This is how Rodin described his companion and model Rose Beuret. For a long time it was thought, wrongly, that she had posed for the *Young Woman in a Flowered Hat* (left) and *Mignon* (right).

Empire, Rodin acquired a more secure position, but at the same time discovered an alien world in which 'the aim is to appeal to the masses, to the detriment of true sculpture'.

Carrier-Belleuse produced a broad selection of work, from architectural ornaments to drawing-room knick-knacks, including busts that were virtually mass-produced; these were inspired by the informal portraits of the 18th century, as he, too, had trained at the Petite Ecole. He was involved in all the important commissions of the period: the Pavillon de Flore, the Grande Galerie of the Louvre, the Paris Opéra....

Rodin participated in these projects, but he quickly began to specialize in producing small-scale, commercialized busts, signed by Carrier-Belleuse. He later maintained: 'Nothing I did then holds any interest for me.'

Nevertheless, his close contact with the successful businessman-sculptor taught him two fundamental lessons: how to organize a large studio employing several people, and how to create infinite variations on a single figure; the same basic figurine modelled in clay could be used nude or draped, decorated with flowers or fruit, with the hair loose or covered by a hat, and could then be translated into plaster, bronze or marble.

In the catalogue of his first Salon, Rodin described himself as a 'pupil of Barye and Carrier-Belleuse'. The latter (above left), though often dismissed as a producer of cheap bric-à-brac, was in fact a talented draughtsman and modeller, who exploited the technical innovations of the 19th century to mass-produce a broad range of items, from small-scale reproductions of larger statues, made of cheap zinc, to *objets de luxe*. Barye (above right) was an animal sculptor who taught at the Museum of Natural History. Rodin visited the basement of the Jardin des Plantes with Barye's son to make studies of the animals.

The Salon rejects *The Man with the Broken Nose*

Rodin had high hopes of his bust of
a model nicknamed Bibi. After his
failure at the Beaux-Arts, the Salon
represented the only chance to escape
from his lowly position as an
architectural sculptor. Crowds poured
in to view this 'battlefield of the artists
of the Second Empire'; it was here that
one could find buyers – the state,
municipalities and wealthy individuals,
who were always strongly influenced by
the official prizes – and here that
reputations were made, 'orchestrated by
that new force in artistic life: the critic'.
The 'Salon piece', which sculptors often
worked on for many months, would
generally be submitted as a plaster cast,
only being executed in more permanent
materials – bronze or marble – after it
had been sold. Rodin's bust of Bibi, the
first work he had submitted to the
Salon, was felt to be too realistic, and
when his name appeared on the list of
the fifty-nine artists whose works had
been rejected, he knew that he was
condemned to several more years
working as an assistant. He was far
more depressed by this rejection than
by his lack of success at the Ecole des Beaux-Arts.

The war years: events take the sculptor to Belgium

Rodin was thirty when the Franco-Prussian War broke
out in 1870. Drafted into the National Guard, he spent
his brief military career, during the siege of Paris, just
waiting, and above all searching for food. Following the
January 1871 surrender, he found himself without work.

In autumn 1870 Carrier-Belleuse, who had been
commissioned to decorate the new Stock Exchange in
Brussels, had moved to the Belgian capital with his

In the 1870s Brussels
was undergoing a
period of transformation
similar to that which
took place in Paris under
the Second Empire.
Rodin helped with the
interior and exterior
decoration of the Stock
Exchange (right), and
also executed caryatids
for some apartment
buildings on the
Boulevard Ansbach.

family and some of his Parisian workforce (including his assistant Joseph van Rasbourg). On hearing of Rodin's predicament, he obtained permission for Rodin to join him in Belgium.

Rodin went alone, leaving Beuret, their son and his father (his mother had died of smallpox during the siege of Paris) in difficult circumstances; Parisians were going hungry, and accommodation was expensive. His aunt Anna took in Jean-Baptiste Rodin, who was beginning to grow senile, and when Beuret went to join her companion in 1872, his aunt also looked after the young Auguste.

The sculptor left behind his studio, with all the clay models that were in progress. As long as she remained in Paris, Beuret was entrusted with the delicate task of draping them regularly in damp cloths, to prevent them from drying out and cracking. From that time on, whenever he was away, Rodin's letters to Beuret ended with the same instructions: 'Take good care of my figure, but don't make it too wet; I'd rather it were slightly firm,' and 'Take a look at the clay models every day.'

Jules Desbois described how, as a young sculptor, he had been visiting Rodin's studio when he saw the bust of Bibi (*The Man with the Broken Nose*, plaster version opposite and marble version left) lying on the floor in a corner. Greatly admiring the piece, he asked the artist whether he would allow him to borrow it for a few days: ' "Take it", he replied with typical generosity. And what modesty! For in spite of his talent, he was a modest, almost timid man ... he was wonderful! The next day I took the bust to the Ecole des Beaux-Arts. "Come and see what I've found," I said to my friends. "Look at this superb antique statue. I've just discovered it in a secondhand dealer's shop." They marvelled at it, and word of it spread from room to room. Everyone came to admire it. And I told them: "Well, Rodin, the man who did this, failed three times to get into the Ecole, and this piece, which you all thought was an antique, was rejected by the Salon." '

Increasingly frustrated by the constraints of his situation, Rodin quarrels with Carrier-Belleuse

In order to earn a little extra money, Rodin spent his evenings modelling female busts, which he attempted to sell under his own name. Carrier-Belleuse was furious, and Rodin was sacked on the spot. There followed several months of penny-pinching, when Rodin found it impossible to send any money to his family, who were by now experiencing the second siege of Paris, under the Commune.

Fortunately, Carrier-Belleuse returned to Paris soon afterwards, leaving work on the Stock Exchange to Van Rasbourg, who suggested to Rodin that they form a partnership; the idea was that Van Rasbourg would sign any works sold in Belgium, while Rodin would design and sign those intended for the French market. Rodin accepted, but continued to work in parallel on his own behalf, selling subjects such as *Suzon* and *Dozia* to the Brussels Compagnie des Bronzes. His association with Van Rasbourg soon became troubled, and they ceased to collaborate after 1875.

It was in Brussels that 'his imagination bore fruit, as he walked to meet his genius'

During his six-year stay in Belgium it became clear to Rodin that there was an artistic world beyond Paris. The French capital ceased to be his unique point of reference, and he felt free to explore other creative paths.

He rediscovered the thirst for knowledge and insatiable curiosity that he had experienced during his time at the Petite Ecole. On Sundays, his only day off, he and Beuret would visit the nearby cathedrals, which fascinated him more and more. In the museums he would stand gazing at Rubens' masterpieces, which in the evening he would paint from memory. Rodin and Beuret would go for long walks together in the forest of Soignes; the poet Rainer Maria Rilke, Rodin's secretary from 1905 to 1906, tells us that Rodin 'would set up his easel anywhere, and paint'. His pockets were stretched quite out of shape by the books he always carried with him; Dante's *Inferno* became his bedtime reading.

Sometimes Rodin combined higgledy-piggledy on the same sheet of paper drawings after the antique, studies of medieval art and even of Michelangelo's work. Part of the mystery of his creative work lies in the way these images are juxtaposed, though the links between them are not always clear.

It was in Brussels that he held his first exhibition, in 1871 – a date that marks his official debut as an independent sculptor.

'The call of Italy, and especially of Michelangelo, becomes irresistible'

Like all artists of the period, Rodin had his sights firmly set on Rome, and he decided to go there in late 1875. He travelled via Rheims, to visit the cathedral, which he found incomparably beautiful.

In a fascinating letter to Beuret he described every detail of his journey: 'You won't be surprised to hear that I have been making a study of Michelangelo ever since I set foot in Florence, and I believe the great magician is beginning to let me into a few of his secrets.' He later explained: 'As my head was full of the Greek models I had studied passionately in the Louvre, I was quite disconcerted by the Michelangelos. At every turn they contradicted the truths I thought I had learnt for ever.' The twisting torsos of Michelangelo were in striking contrast to the calm balance of antique statues. Everywhere he went Rodin made notes and sketches.

The first scandal: Rodin exhibits *The Age of Bronze*

On his return to Brussels Rodin tackled with renewed enthusiasm a large-scale statue intended for the Paris Salon, on which he had been working since the summer of 1875. His model, Auguste Neyt, a Belgian soldier, later described how difficult it had been to find the right pose; Rodin was very demanding and was determined to avoid the exaggerated musculature of conventional poses.

The Age of Bronze was presented to the Cercle Artistique de Bruxelles. In the face of such perfection, an anonymous article – ostensibly written in praise of the sculpture – made the insidious suggestion that it had been cast from life, a technique unworthy of a true sculptor. By the time Rodin submitted the plaster cast of the statue to the jury of the Paris Salon a few months later, rumours had already spread. Rodin tried to defend himself; 'I would need a mind more cunning than my own to find a way out of all these difficulties,' he complained. He collected letters of support from Belgian

Photograph of Auguste Neyt in the pose of *The Age of Bronze* (above). Centre: The plaster cast exhibited in Brussels and Paris. Right: The bronze later bought by the state.

artists, together with photographs and casts of the live model, so that the jury could compare them with the statue. His efforts were wasted; the jury never even opened the envelope, let alone the crates of casts which Rodin had had made at great expense. For the first time Rodin encountered the power of the press; he learned to fear journalists and never to forget what they could do.

" *The Man with the Broken Nose* had revealed how Rodin could find his way around a face; *The Age of Bronze* proved his unlimited mastery over the body."
Rainer Maria Rilke

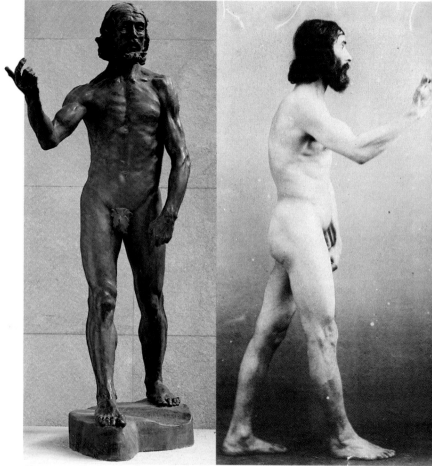

Return to Paris: 'the future looks bleak'

After this *succès de scandale* Rodin was keen to return
to Paris. He no longer knew anyone there, however, so
Fourquet negotiated his third 'rehabilitation' into the
Carrier-Belleuse workshop. He travelled to Paris via the
cathedrals of Amiens, Noyon, Soissons and Rheims, and
at the end of 1877 he moved into lodgings in the Rue
Saint-Jacques with Beuret, their son and his father.

"One morning there
was a knock at the door
of my studio.... It was
a peasant from the
Abruzzi who had come
to offer his services as a
model.... He made me
think immediately of St
John the Baptist ... a
visionary, a believer."

Rodin then began to do freelance work for the Sèvres porcelain manufactory, where Carrier-Belleuse, who had been appointed art director, was keen to develop the sculptural side of production. This work provided only a small, supplementary income, and so Rodin accepted anything else that came his way, working in Nice, Marseilles and Strasbourg. The Paris International Exhibition of 1878 was a godsend for Rodin, as for all the craftsmen of the age. He was hired by the workshop of Eugène Legrain to produce the decorations for the Trocadéro fountain.

It was during this period that he created one of his most powerful figures: *St John the Baptist*, which was exhibited in 1880 with *The Age of Bronze*. He later used the studies for this sculpture to create the astonishing large male figure that the critics spontaneously nicknamed *The Walking Man* in 1907.

Rodin submitted entries for several of the competitions to design monuments organized by the state and municipalities, but without success. Only his statue of *Jean d'Alembert* was accepted to decorate the façade of the new Hôtel de Ville, which had been rebuilt following the Commune. Nevertheless, his skill was becoming legendary and was the talk of the ateliers. He claimed to be able to model a whole human figure in only a few hours. And thanks to the recognition of some of his peers, who had come to his defence during *The Age of Bronze* affair, Rodin was accepted into Parisian artistic circles.

"The man undressed, then climbed on to the revolving stand as if he had never posed before; he planted himself firmly on his feet, his head up and body erect, with his weight supported equally by both legs, which were open like a pair of compasses. The stance was so perfect, so straightforward, so true that I cried out: 'But that's a man walking!' I resolved to copy straight away what I had seen."
Rodin

The Walking Man (left) is one of the truncated statues, of which Rilke said: 'Nothing essential is lacking. Each one appears as a complete whole that will allow of no further addition.'

"One moment he showed the agony of sensuality, the next he exalted it; he could express the pain of life and the terror of death, and of hell itself; in *The Burghers of Calais* he was the voice of history; in *Victor Hugo* he showed the elements in turmoil; in *Balzac* he was the multiplicity of humanity."

So wrote the critic Octave Mirbeau of Rodin during the 1880s, when Rodin's creativity and capacity for work seemed without limit.

CHAPTER 3

"HE IS BEYOND ALL MEASURE"

"Wandering amongst these thousands of objects ... you find yourself turning involuntarily towards the two hands from which this world was born."
Rainer Maria Rilke

Despite the controversy surrounding *The Age of Bronze* and *St John the Baptist*, Edmond Turquet, under-secretary at the Ministry of Fine Arts, persuaded of Rodin's talent by several respected sculptors, including Carrier-Belleuse, Jean-Alexandre Falguière and Paul Dubois, purchased these works for the Musée du Luxembourg. Furthermore, to underline his independence from the all-powerful Institut, Turquet commissioned in 1880 Rodin, a little-known but already highly controversial figure, to fulfil a large-scale public project intended for the future Museum of Decorative Arts: a doorway, decorated with bas-reliefs based on Dante's *Divine Comedy*.

It seems it was Rodin himself who chose the subject, having at last found an opportunity to draw on the work that had obsessed him for so many years. He argued for an ambitious plan, explaining that the multitude of small figures of which the work would be composed would put an end, once and for all, to accusations that he cast his sculptures from life.

References to the Florentine writer's works were common during this period: Eugène Delacroix had painted *Dante and Virgil Crossing the Styx*; Honoré de Balzac's series of novels *La Comédie Humaine* was a clear reference to the *Divine Comedy*; and Carpeaux had sculpted an *Ugolino*, which had made quite an impression on Rodin. What was unusual about Rodin's project was his desire to create a three-dimensional vision

The first design for *The Gates of Hell*, with the division into eight panels, was inspired by Lorenzo Ghiberti's doors for the Baptistry in Florence. Later on, Rodin was guided more by the association of the forms than by the logic of the architectural structure.

of the work as a whole, which would teem with individual characters and scenes.

First he must find a studio large enough to house the project; it has to be at least 6 m high

The Dépôt des Marbres, at 182 Rue de l'Université, was where blocks of marble were stored before being delivered to sculptors working on state-sponsored projects; it also included twelve studios. From 1880 Rodin shared one of these with Joseph Osbach, and he was eventually allowed to use two adjoining ateliers. Although Rodin later had other studios, some of them

T*he Mask of Minos* (above), a powerful study for *The Gates of Hell.*

"Amongst the commissions are some monumental doors, for which the sculptor Rodin is at present finishing his studies.... Those who have admired, in the artist's studio, the finished sketches [Left: The third clay study for *The Gates*] and the ones on which he is still working, are unanimous in declaring that these doors will be the most important work of the century.... Auguste Rodin is virtually unknown.... There are particular reasons for this. Rodin is a great artist. He detests coteries and moves little in society.... He is happy just to produce masterpieces that are admired by his friends, and which posterity, which is never wrong, has already marked with its eternal stamp of approval."

Octave Mirbeau

still more vast, he always retained the one on the Rue de l'Université, and this was the address that appeared on his writing paper.

The admiring visitors who came in droves every Saturday wondered how the artist managed to find his way around all the arms and legs belonging to the various figures in his *Hell*, which lay scattered over tables, shelves and even on the ground.

'Dante is not only a visionary and a writer; he is also a sculptor'

'For a whole year I lived with Dante, with him alone, drawing the eight circles of his *Inferno*. At the end of this year I realized that my drawings had become too remote from reality; so I started all over again, working from nature, with my models.' The hundreds of drawings Rodin produced, in Chinese ink, shaded with a brown ink wash to help anticipate their sculptural effect, are in fact commentaries on, rather than illustrations of, Dante's masterpiece.

The work quickly took on a more general significance. Although certain figures are drawn directly from Dante – *Paolo and Francesca*, *Ugolino* and *The Thinker*, which represents the poet himself – Rodin rapidly went beyond the subject matter, introducing figures that suggest Baudelairean influence. But his aims were far broader even than this; he wanted to create an entire universe, to paint the feelings and passions of all humanity.

Once he had defined the dimensions of *The Gates*, he constructed a huge wooden framework, which he covered first with clay, then with plaster, and on which he arranged his panels in

Rodin was already 'abused by mediocrity and persecuted by the hatred of fools' (above).

low and high relief, his individual figures and groups of figures sculpted virtually in the round.

For twenty years he wrestles with *The Gates*, without ever completing them

The master could never resist the thrill of creation; nothing was finalized. He was constantly improvising, inserting yet another small figure amongst the others, then moving it, and if necessary breaking it up so as to re-use the pieces for further experiments.

The Gates could not hold all the sculptures he wanted to include. The countless figures, which illustrate the gradual development of his inspiration, constitute a 'diary of his life as a sculptor'.

"The more points of contact two bodies offered to each other, the more impatiently they rushed towards each other like two closely related chemical bodies, and the more the new unity that they formed became tightly welded together, forming an organic whole."
Rainer Maria Rilke

"He is a man with common features, a fleshy nose, bright eyes flashing beneath unhealthily red lids, a long yellow beard, hair cut short and brushed back, and a round head, a head suggesting gentle, stubborn obstinacy – a man such as I imagine Christ's disciples looked like."
Jules and Edmond de Goncourt, *Journal*, April 1878

The Gates of Hell

"He endowed hundreds
of figures that were
barely larger than his
hand with the life of
every passion, the
flowering of every
pleasure and the weight
of every vice. He created
bodies that touched each
other all over and clung
together like animals
that have sunk their
teeth into each other,
and fell like a single
living organism into
the abyss; bodies that
listened like faces, that
took flight like arms
raised to hurl
something, chains of
bodies, garlands and
vine tendrils, and heavy
clusters of human forms
in which the sap of sin
rose from the roots of
pain."
Rainer Maria Rilke

Lefthand lintel of *The
Gates* (opposite).
This page, clockwise
from top left: *The Three
Shades, The Prodigal
Son, Fugit Amor* and
The Falling Man. Above:
Plaster cast of *The Gates*.

The Thinker

"He sits, silently lost in contemplation, heavy with thoughts and images; he thinks with all his strength – with the strength of a man who acts. His whole body has become head and the very blood of his veins has become brain."

Rainer Maria Rilke

Over two hundred figures, arranged with no symmetrical pattern, flow one into the other, creating an intertwining, tangled mass. Rodin was trapped in the dizzying whirlpool of his own fertile imagination.

He subsequently eliminated several of these figures, and in the plaster model exhibited in 1900 almost all of the figures modelled in the round had been removed. On the sculptor's death *The Gates* were reassembled by the first director of the Musée Rodin, Léonce Bénédite. They were first cast in bronze in 1926, for the Rodin Museum in Philadelphia.

'*The Gates of Hell* is full of masterpieces', proclaims Antoine Bourdelle, a sculptor and friend of Rodin

In fact, the various figures from *The Gates* have become recognized as masterpieces in their own right: *The Thinker, The Three Shades, Despair, The Crouching Woman, She who was Once the Helmet-maker's Beautiful Wife, Ugolino, Adam and Eve, I am Beautiful, Fugit Amor, Kneeling Fauness....*

The Italian woman who posed for *Eve* (opposite above) had not told Rodin that she was pregnant, so the sculptor had to modify his work continually. Opposite below: *Ugolino* devouring his sons. Left: The large figure of *Adam,* which, together with *Eve,* frames *The Gates of Hell. She who was Once the Helmetmaker's Beautiful Wife* (above) can be compared with Jules Desbois' *Poverty* and Camille Claudel's *Old Helmetmaker's Wife.*

Some of these figures provided the raw material for daring new combinations, and thus gave rise to new sculptures. *The Prodigal Son, Paolo and Francesca, Fugit Amor* and *Despair,* for example, all evolved from one of *Ugolino*'s sons. Any figure could be enlarged or reduced, and translated, on whatever scale, into plaster, marble or bronze. Moreover, all these parts of bodies from *The Gates* provided Rodin with a reservoir of forms on which he drew to the very end of his life.

The sculptor is now highly sought after amongst the smart Parisian set of the 1880s

No one can lead a successful career without becoming involved in society. Though shy and morbidly anxious, Rodin nevertheless did what was expected of him. He was to be seen in fashionable salons: that of Madame Charpentier, who received the Goncourt brothers, Alphonse Daudet, Joris-Karl Huysmans and Emile Zola, or that of Juliette Adam – a more political milieu – where he would have met Léon Gambetta and Pierre Waldeck-Rousseau. The sculptor, who was still not particularly well off, wore paper collars and cuffs, on which he scribbled down any ideas that came to him, so as not to forget them.

Several critics used their skill to promote his art: Emile Bergerat, who claimed to be the first journalist to have met him; Octave Mirbeau, whose attachment to the sculptor became the subject of a famous satirical song: 'Rodin is great, Mirbeau is his prophet'; the critic Gustave Geoffroy; Léon Gauchez, editor of the magazine *L'Art*; Edmond Bazire, a journalist on the periodical

Above from left to right: Antonin Proust, minister of fine arts, then president of the Union Centrale des Arts Décoratifs, a politician who consistently supported Rodin; Roger Marx, man of letters and art critic; the painter Jean-Paul Laurens; the sculptor Jules Dalou, a fellow student at the Petite Ecole; the critic Octave Mirbeau, an impassioned and ardent admirer; Albert-Ernest Carrier-Belleuse; Pierre Puvis de Chavannes, painter and great friend of Rodin; Madame Vicuña, the wife of a Chilean diplomat, whose bust was enthusiastically received at the 1888 Salon. Opposite: Rodin in 1887.

L'Intransigeant; and many others. During this period Rodin also made several trips to England to stay with his friend Legros, who taught him engraving and introduced him into English artistic circles.

While working on *The Gates,* the sculptor produces a host of busts

The portrait busts Rodin executed during the 1880s confirmed his reputation. Most of them were produced as marks of friendship or thanks. In fact, the artist preferred modelling portraits of his friends to carrying out more remunerative commissions. He felt better able to demonstrate the full extent of his talents when he was not bound by financial obligation. Then, as Rilke tells us: 'A man's face is to him like a dramatic scene in which he himself takes part; he is right in the heart of it, and nothing that happens there escapes him or is indifferent to him.... He wishes to know nothing, except what he sees. And he sees everything.' He made busts of Legros, Carrier-Belleuse, Jules Dalou, Henri Becque, W. E. Henley, Antonin Proust, Omer Dewavrin, mayor of Calais, Octave Mirbeau, Roger Marx, Madame Alfred Roll and countless others.

Edmond Bazire advised him to consolidate his reputation by executing the bust of a famous man. He suggested two figures whom he knew well: the novelist Victor Hugo and the

"A fine bust reveals the moral and physical reality of the sitter, expresses the secret thoughts, probes the innermost recesses of the soul, the strengths and weaknesses; all masks drop.... Purely through sensitivity, the artist becomes an enlightener, a soothsayer."

Rodin

political journalist Henri Rochefort. Victor Hugo, who felt that 'after David d'Angers ... no one could do his bust', declined to sit for Rodin. However, he did allow Rodin to visit him, provided that the artist agreed to abide by his conditions: 'I worked for hours on the veranda of his house, which was full of flowers and green plants. Occasionally, I would see Victor Hugo cross the drawing-room, a cold, hard expression on his face; he would go and sit down at the far end of the room, self-absorbed, thoughtful.... You know that I make it a principle to work by comparing the various profile views of any work with those of the living model. As I could not follow my usual procedure in this case, I would go and stand beside or behind him, following him with my gaze, making rapid sketches of him, drawing as many profiles as I could on small squares of paper; he did not even look at me; but was kind enough not to ask me to leave; he put up with me. I made several outline drawings of his skull, which I then compared with the profiles of the bust; that is how I managed to execute it, but only with great difficulty. I did the best I could.'

In the studio: models, casters, pointers and *praticiens*

Rodin's studio was organized like a factory where division of labour is the guiding principle. The plaster

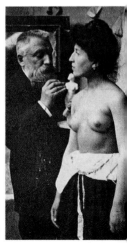

"In front of the model, I work with the same desire to copy the truth as if I were making a portrait; I do not correct nature, I incorporate myself into her; she leads me. I can only work from a model. The sight of the human form fortifies and nourishes me."

Rodin

Rodin with a model in 1895 (opposite, below right). The other pictures are of Victor Hugo – sketches, plaster and bronze busts, and an etching.

caster produced copies of the clay originals modelled by the sculptor; the pointer rough-hewed the marble blocks and drilled the reference points that would enable the *praticien*, or assistant, to carve a copy of the plaster model. The bronze-caster would work independently for several artists, and the patination of the bronzes would be carried out by a patinater, who might also be independent – like Limet, who worked for Rodin around 1900. The model was another important member of the studio, and Rodin was very particular: he preferred untrained models, because they did not automatically adopt conventional poses.

The sculptor worked simultaneously on his commissioned projects, his own experiments and portrait busts, which he produced in great numbers. He drew up lists of collaborators, permanent or occasional, which, by 1900, had become very impressive.

Unlike other sculptors, he did not surround himself simply with craftsmen, but sought out individuals who showed promise, such as Jules Desbois, François Pompon, Camille Claudel, Aristide Maillol and Antoine Bourdelle. He made his position clear: 'I do not have any pupils, but I could take you on as an assistant.'

Camille Claudel, a young sculptor

It was late in 1883 that Rodin first met Camille Claudel, while standing in for his friend Alfred Boucher at a class he gave to a group of young women. The elder sister of the future playwright and diplomat Paul Claudel, Camille was then nineteen, and in spite of her family's strong opposition, she wanted to become a sculptor.

During the five years that Camille Claudel (above) spent working in the master's studio, Rodin consulted her opinion on all kinds of matters, and used her as a model; in his will he stipulated that a room in the Hôtel Biron should be set aside for her sculptures. Left: A plaster bust of Claudel, with one of *The Burghers'* hands attached to it. Right: *Thought*, 'this transcendent vision of life, which rises slowly from the heavy sleep of the stone' (Rilke).

'That embrace in which there is both desire and chastity'

"The man's head is bent, that of the woman is lifted, and their mouths meet in a kiss that seals the intimate union of their two beings. Through the extraordinary magic of art, this kiss, which is scarcely indicated by the meeting of their lips, is clearly visible, not only in their meditative expressions, but still more in the shiver that runs equally through both bodies, from the nape of the neck to the soles of the feet, in every fibre of the man's back, as it bends, straightens, grows still, where everything adores – bones, muscles, nerves, flesh – in his leg, which seems to twist slowly, as if moving to brush against his lover's leg; and in the woman's feet, which hardly touch the ground, uplifted with her whole being as she is swept away with ardour and grace."

Gustave Geffroy

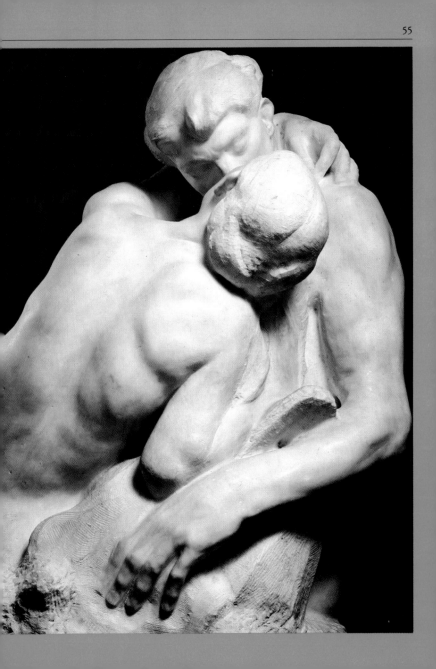

Struck by her freshness, the originality of her talent and her fierce desire to succeed, Rodin was soon captivated. He found in her an ideal lover and work companion, with whom he could discuss matters on an equal footing. He clearly retained a great deal of affection for Rose Beuret, but she had been unable to adapt to the change in his social standing.

For her part, 'Mademoiselle Camille', as he called her, had found a man much older than herself, for whom she had intense admiration. From 1885 she was the master's assistant. One sign of the confidence he placed in her is that he gave her studies to do, the hands and feet of the large-scale compositions on which he was working. 'The modelling of clay had long ceased to hold any secrets for her; she tempered plaster as nobody else could, and carved marble with an energy and precision that the master himself never acquired.' She worked alongside the animal-sculptor François Pompon, who was then in charge of Rodin's atelier, and who witnessed their romance, but also their frequent arguments.

The face and body of 'Mademoiselle Camille'

Until 1888 Claudel continued to live with her parents, who were completely unaware of her liaison. Then she moved to 113 Boulevard d'Italie, near the Clos-Payen, also known as the Folie-Neubourg, which Rodin had just begun renting. It was in this magnificent, though half-ruined 18th-century residence, surrounded by a neglected garden, that the two artists worked together and carried on their secret love affair.

The face and body of Claudel haunt Rodin's oeuvre. She is *Thought, Aurora, St George, France, The Convalescent.* Several of the damned souls in *The Gates of Hell* were modelled on her. Her presence changed the

Fully aware of Claudel's talent, Rodin declared: 'I showed her where to find gold, but the gold she discovered was well and truly her own.' *Aurora* (left) was modelled on her. Below: Claudel with a sculpture.

way he looked at women, who came to occupy an important place in his work.

It was during this period that he glorified the loving couple. *The Eternal Idol, The Kiss, Eternal Springtime, Paolo and Francesca, L'Emprise (Ascendancy), Fugit Amor:* in all these sculptures produced between 1885 and 1896, the movement of the modelled bodies expresses passion, love, the heights of ecstasy and the depths of suffering. Without a doubt Rodin created some of the most erotic and often the most daring sculptural images ever known: such as *The Crouching Woman, I am Beautiful, L'Emprise, Iris, Messenger of the Gods, The Damned Women....*

That colossal evocation of history: *The Burghers of Calais*

In 1884 a national subscription was launched at the instigation of the mayor of Calais, Omer Dewavrin, to erect a monument in honour of Eustache de Saint-Pierre, hero of the city – and Rodin was asked to design it. While reading the version of events in Jean Froissart's *Chronicles*, he discovered that there was, in fact, not one hero, but several. He was immediately seduced by the subject, in which he found much to inspire him. He decided to represent all six burghers of Calais, and wrote to the committee: 'I have been lucky enough to hit on an idea

"The woman's head leans forward slightly; with an expression of indulgence, pride and patience, she gazes down, as if from the height of a still night, upon the man, who sinks his head into her breast as if into a wealth of flowers. He, too, is kneeling, but lower down, kneeling deep into the stone. His hands lie stretched out behind him, like useless, empty objects.... There is something of the mood of purgatory alive within this work. Heaven is near, but has not yet been attained, hell is close, but has not yet been forgotten."
Rainer Maria Rilke's description of *The Eternal Idol*

that appeals to me, and which would be original in its execution.' He explained: 'Don't worry; your money will be well spent; for you don't often find such a fine idea and opportunity to excite feelings of patriotism and self-sacrifice.'

The jury were pleased with the first rough sketch, but were less enthusiastic about the second maquette, presented to them in July 1885: 'This is not how we imagine our glorious fellow citizens. Their dejected attitudes conflict with our vision.' Yet, with the support of Dewavrin, Rodin continued to work on the group.

'First, I usually create my stone children without clothes'

Rodin modelled the six figures separately, and, in accordance with academic tradition, they were modelled nude before being clothed. 'Then all I have to do is throw some drapery over them, and wherever it clings, the model becomes vibrant with life; it is flesh and blood, not some cold effigy.' In 1886, just as Rodin was about to undertake the execution and casting of the monument, the project was suspended because of financial difficulties. The committee was disbanded, so Rodin was able to complete the work just as he pleased.

Jean Froissart tells us that in 1347, during the siege of Calais, King Edward III agreed to spare the population of the town on condition that six of the most important citizens leave Calais, bareheaded and barefoot, with a rope around their necks, and carrying the keys to the town and castle. The first maquette submitted by Rodin (left) portrayed them as a group.

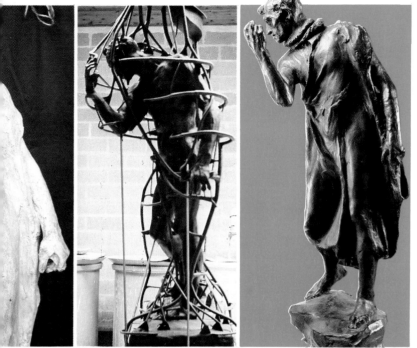

He had to rent a stable on the Rue Saint-Jacques to store the six *Burghers*, until their unveiling in 1895.

The 1880s end with honours

Rodin became a Chevalier of the Légion d'honneur and a founder member of the Société Nationale des Beaux-Arts. The state commissioned him to create a monument to the painter Claude Lorraine, and another to Victor Hugo, for which he submitted two designs.

The centenary of the French Revolution, 1889, was the year the Eiffel Tower was built for the International Exhibition. But the artistic event of the year was a joint exhibition by Rodin and Claude Monet, held at the Georges Petit gallery. Monet sent seventy paintings, and Rodin exhibited thirty-two plaster casts. The two artists – each an innovator in his own sphere – remained friends throughout their lives.

Rodin created each *Burgher* as a separate, freestanding figure with its own base, so that he was free to move them about independently, like pawns on a chessboard. Opposite, above left: *Jean d'Aire*, undraped. Above, from left to right: *Pierre de Wissant*, cast in plaster, then imprisoned in a network of channels for bronze-casting, and finally as a finished statue. The group of *Burghers* was first shown at the joint Monet-Rodin exhibition.

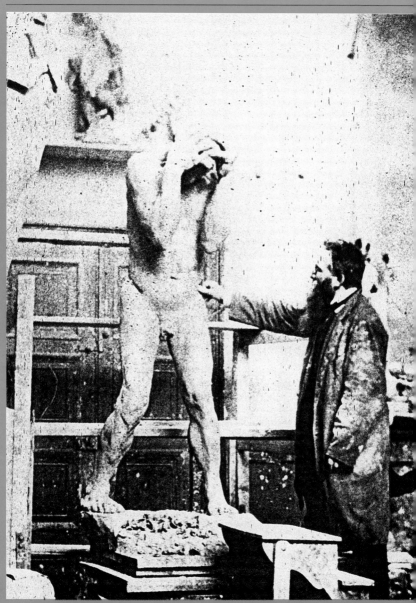

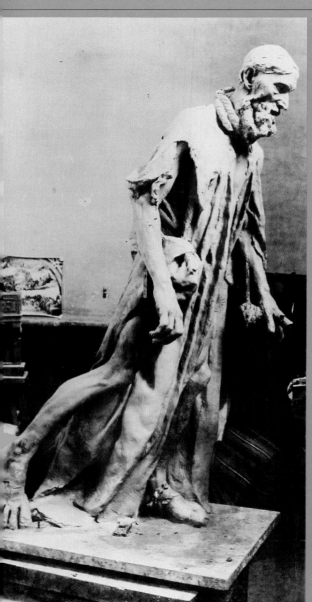

**Postures and states
of mind**

Rodin modelling the
nude figure of
Pierre d'Andrieu (far
left). The clay model of
Eustache de Saint-Pierre
(left), draped, on its base
and (above) in a
photograph retouched
by Rodin. The sculptor
kept up a voluminous
correspondence with the
mayor of Calais, to keep
him informed of the
progress of the work. 'I
have finished my nudes,
that is, the underneath
part. You will see that
what is finished, though
it is the bit one does not
see, is the most
important part.'

" **I**f truth is doomed to die, my *Balzac* will be destroyed by later generations. But if truth is eternal, I predict that my statue will gain acceptance. This work, which people laughed at, which they were careful to mock because they could not destroy it, is the product of my entire life, the mainspring of my aesthetic. From the day I created it, I became a new man."

CHAPTER 4

"TRUE GREATNESS LIES IN SIMPLIFICATION"

The statue of *Balzac*, rejected and withdrawn from the Salon, is an imposing presence in the garden at Meudon. In its place the Société des Gens de Lettres commissioned another sculpture from Jean-Alexandre Falguière, seen on the left in this caricature.

'Thanks to you I am now the sculptor of Balzac...'

'I find myself employed in a formidable manner. I will therefore do my best to be worthy of the commission.' In this letter of 9 July 1891 Rodin expressed his gratitude to Emile Zola, then president of the Société des Gens de Lettres, who had proposed and supported his nomination. The society wished to honour its founder, Honoré de Balzac. Rodin proposed to create a monument 3 m high, to be delivered in May 1893 and erected on the Place du Palais-Royal.

It was a real challenge to represent someone of Balzac's stature, both figuratively and literally. Rodin threw himself into the search for anything that might help to conjure up an image of the novelist. 'In the library in Paris there are seven or eight lithographs of Balzac, but they are small. I have had photographed a very fine pastel portrait by Court, which is in the Tours museum, where there is also a drawing by Boulanger ... I have also studied death masks and important documents relating to his life.' He travelled to Brussels to see the cast of Balzac's hand, and is said to have exclaimed: 'Now I have everything I need. With this hand, I will rebuild Balzac.'

He called upon his friends. The photographer Nadar gave him a daguerreotype; the woman of letters Aurel sent him a postcard of a Balzac-shaped rock, and Gustave Geffroy located a bookseller on the Boulevard Saint-Germain who looked just like him. Several works on Balzac can be found in Rodin's library. All this documentary material helped Rodin to familiarize himself with Balzac's physical form and personality – but it was not enough.

"For years and years Rodin's whole life was completely absorbed by this figure. He visited Balzac's native country and saw the landscapes of the Touraine which frequently make their appearance in Balzac's novels; he read his letters, he studied the remaining portraits of Balzac, and he continually re-read his works.... Fired with the spirit of Balzac, Rodin began to model the external appearance of the writer."
Rainer Maria Rilke

"As form followed form, Rodin's vision slowly grew. And at last he saw Balzac: a substantial figure, striding powerfully forwards, its heaviness counteracted by the fall of the coat. The hair weighed down on the powerful neck, and from the mass of hair there gazed a face intoxicated with its own vision, a face that boiled with creative energy: the face of an elemental force. This was Balzac in all the fullness of his productive powers, the founder of generations, the waster of fates.... This was how Rodin saw Balzac in a moment of intense concentration and tragic exaggeration, and this was how he created him. The vision did not fade; it came into being."

Rainer Maria Rilke

'Even with all the documents, you can never forge nature'

Rodin openly admitted that he could not work without a model, and that when he had nothing to copy, he had not the first idea how to proceed.

He returned to Anjou, where he had been every summer since 1887 with Camille Claudel. This time the aim was not just to spend some time away from it all with his 'pupil', but to find a model for the statue in the writer's native region. He discovered a postman who strongly resembled Balzac, and made a series of studies of him on the spot. To recreate the overall appearance, he found Balzac's old tailor, had a frock coat made to his measurements, dipped it in plaster, then left it to dry on an upright dummy. As usual, he first made three-dimensional nude studies of the figure, to be sure of the anatomy. He also modelled heads, busts, trunks; he made studies of Balzac in a monk's habit, in a dressing gown, without a head.

'Don't they understand that great art does not keep to delivery dates'

Rodin worked feverishly, but took far longer than the time originally allowed. The Société des Gens de Lettres became impatient and in October 1894 demanded that the statue be delivered within twenty-four hours. The sculptor replied, via the press, asking to be allowed to finish the monument 'in an atmosphere of calm reflection and freedom, which are the only conditions under which a work of art can be produced'. The quarrel grew increasingly bitter. The society's new president, Jean Aicard, who supported Rodin, resigned. The sculptor offered to deposit at the Caisse des Dépôts the 10,000 francs that had been paid to him, until delivery had been made, which he judged possible within the year.

On the 19 August 1896 the newspaper *Le Temps* announced that, having executed numerous maquettes, Rodin had finished his studies: 'Balzac will be shown standing, in a simple but powerful pose, with his legs a little apart and his arms crossed. He will be wearing a form of long dressing gown without a belt, which falls to the floor.' Opposite: M. Lapret, one of the models for *Balzac*'s face, with a nude maquette and sketches.

Georges Clemenceau and Gustave Geffroy took Rodin's part. Zola, who was abroad at the time, reminded him: 'Balzac is waiting, and his glory should not suffer for too much longer through your legitimate concern for your own reputation.'

Rodin decides to exhibit a plaster cast of his *Balzac* at the 1898 Salon. After the *vernissage* the society refuses to accept the statue

'The committee of the Société des Gens de Lettres feels it sadly incumbent upon it to protest at the rough model exhibited at the Salon by Monsieur Rodin and declines to recognize it as a statue of Balzac.' This text was released to the press. The committee took back the 10,000 francs and awarded the commission to Falguière instead.

Friends and admirers of Rodin, from every walk of life, composed a letter of protest and launched a fund. Since 1896 France had been divided by the Dreyfus affair, and almost all of those who supported the *Balzac* were Dreyfusards. Rodin, who began to fear that this dispute might be taken out of the context of art and dragged into the more dangerous realm of politics, refused all these interventions on his behalf. In an open letter he wrote: 'It is my firm wish to retain sole possession of my work.' He withdrew the *Balzac* from the Salon, announcing that it would not be erected anywhere. He did not have the statue cast in bronze, and installed the plaster in the garden of his house at Meudon. To avoid further repercussions of the scandal, he even refused to exhibit the statue in Brussels, in spite of appeals for it to be shown there. Whenever the artist felt he had been misunderstood, he turned in on himself completely, waiting for time to prove him right:

The pro-*Balzac* camp included many artists and writers, including the poet Stéphane Mallarmé (above) and Claude Monet, who wrote to Rodin: 'Let them protest all they like, you have never achieved so much before.' The argument went beyond artistic circles, and the passions of the general public were aroused. The *Balzac*, presented to the Salon in 1898 (opposite), was described as an obese monster, a shapeless lump and a giant foetus.

Cordialement à vous mon cher ami. Claude Monet

'What does it matter?' he wrote. 'My *Balzac* will find its way into people's minds, either by force or by persuasion.'

Rodin's relationship with Claudel comes to an end

The *Balzac* was not delayed purely because of the time it took for Rodin's creative ideas to mature. He was also finding it difficult to cope with his separation from Claudel, and complained to everyone that he was suffering from anaemia. He often turned down invitations.

In 1893 Claudel returned to live at 113 Boulevard d'Italie. Without making a complete break from Rodin, she ceased to cohabit with him. She had long hoped that they would be married, but Rodin refused to give up his long-term companion Rose Beuret. In 1893 Rodin left his insalubrious lodgings on the Rue des Grands-Augustins, and moved, with Beuret, first to the Chemin Scribe at Bellevue, then to the Villa des Brillants on the slopes of Meudon.

He was still very much in love with 'Mlle Camille' and redoubled his attentions to her in an attempt to maintain the ties that she was determined to loosen. Even after their separation, he continued to support her and intervene on her behalf, acting always through a

After his separation from Camille Claudel (left), Rodin lived from 1896 with Rose Beuret (right) in the Villa des Brillants (below) in Meudon. He added to it the façade of the Château d'Issy, which he had rescued from demolition, and the Pavillon de l'Alma, which was reconstructed in the grounds there after the retrospective exhibition of 1900.

third party, because she refused to accept any help that came from him. At the Salon of 1892 he had asked the president of the jury to assure that her bust of him would be displayed with suitable prominence: 'I would not raise this question again on my own account, but it is my duty to defend the interests of a young artist whose true talent so justly deserves our eager concern.' In 1895 he asked the scholar Gabriel Mourey, as a friend, to do 'something for this genius of a woman (no exaggeration) whom I love so dearly'. He sometimes paid Claudel's assistant, as she was constantly short of money. In 1898 the journalist Mathias Morhardt wrote a long article about Claudel in *Le Mercure d'art*. Her reputation grew, and she exhibited *La Petite Châtelaine*, *The Waltz*, *The Gossips*, *The Wave*, *Clotho* and *L'Age mûr* – her most autobiographical work – at the Salon.

Claudel's moods are unpredictable. The first symptoms of a persecution complex appear

She accused Rodin of stealing one of her marble statues, and threatened him: 'Just make sure you keep well away from my studio.' There was a strong similarity in style between the two artists during the early years of their life together. Claudel had been both the muse and the right hand of Rodin. She had shared her talents with him without a moment's thought, and in certain works, such as *The Young Girl and the Grass* and *Galatea*, it is impossible to determine which of them inspired the other. When they separated, Claudel felt dispossessed. It seemed to her that her vital energies had been sapped, that Rodin had fed on her genius. Rodin's career was progressing effortlessly, while she had enormous difficulty in shaking off the label of 'Rodin's pupil' and was sinking into obscurity.

From 1905 these obsessions took on a psychotic character. According to the few people whom she still saw, her health deteriorated and she began to behave oddly. She would destroy in the summer everything she

Rose Beuret fearfully put up with all the humiliations and infidelities inflicted on her by the man she never ceased to call 'Monsieur Rodin'. Camille Claudel, however, refused to share him or to be dependent on him. She wanted the master for

herself alone, just as she was determined to owe her artistic success to nobody but herself. Rodin was very pleased with the bust she made of him *c.* 1888 (above).

had carved the previous winter and would disappear for months at a time, leaving no address. In 1913, the year of her father's death, Camille Claudel was confined in Ville-Evrard, then in Montdevergues, where she lived for a further thirty years. She died in the communal room of the asylum at Villeneuve-lès-Avignon.

Claude Lorraine, The Burghers of Calais, Victor Hugo: the final episode

Rodin produced far fewer works during this decade. Nevertheless, *Balzac* did not absorb all his time and energy. In 1892, after several arguments, the monument to *Claude Lorraine*, which had been commissioned in 1889, was unveiled in Nancy.

Omer Dewavrin, the mayor of Calais, at last succeeded in bringing *The Burghers of Calais* project to a satisfactory conclusion. But the choice of pedestal raised fresh arguments. Rodin wanted either a very high base, like that of Andrea del Verrochio's *Colleoni* statue in Venice, so that the group would stand out against a backdrop of open sky, or a 'very low base, so that the public can see into the very heart of the subject'. The committee decided on a compromise solution, 'which

The Burghers outlined against the sky at Meudon, erected on a very high scaffolding platform, as Rodin would have preferred them to appear in the Calais monument.

was supposed to please everyone, including me', Rodin commented somewhat bitterly.

The monument was unveiled on the 15 June 1895, in the presence of his friends Octave Mirbeau, Roger Marx, Gustave Geffroy, and with all the usual attractions typical of celebrations under the Third Republic: gymnastic competitions, a brass band parade, an ascent by hot-air balloons, banquets and speeches. Only in 1924 were *The Burghers* moved to the Place d'Armes and installed on a low base, level with their fellow citizens.

In 1889 the sculptor was commissioned to produce a *Victor Hugo* for the Panthéon. As he represented the great man of letters seated and nude, Rodin's design was rejected. In June 1891 he did another *Victor Hugo*. The plaster model was not shown until 1897, and the marble monument was unveiled in 1909 at the Palais-Royal.

The *Victor Hugo* monument, showing the writer with his muse (below), was exhibited in its entirety at the Salon of 1897. In 1906 Rodin decided to remove *The Tragic Muse* and *Meditation* from the group, and to explore these figures as separate sculptures. The official unveiling of the monument (below left) took place on the 30 September 1909.

"**I** am convinced that by showing 'my sculpture' and demonstrating what I understand by sculpture, I will be rendering some service to the cause of art." After the *Balzac* affair and the painful break with Camille Claudel, Rodin made a new beginning. He was at last financially secure and able to promote his work. He used his remaining strength to create a museum bringing together all his sculptures and other collections.

CHAPTER 5

"THE FAME THAT HE ACHIEVED..."

A rare colour photograph of 1907 (left). *The Cathedral* (right).

"Rodin was solitary before fame came to him. And the fame that he achieved rendered him perhaps more solitary than ever. For fame is ultimately nothing more than the sum of misunderstandings that crystallize around a new name."

Rainer Maria Rilke

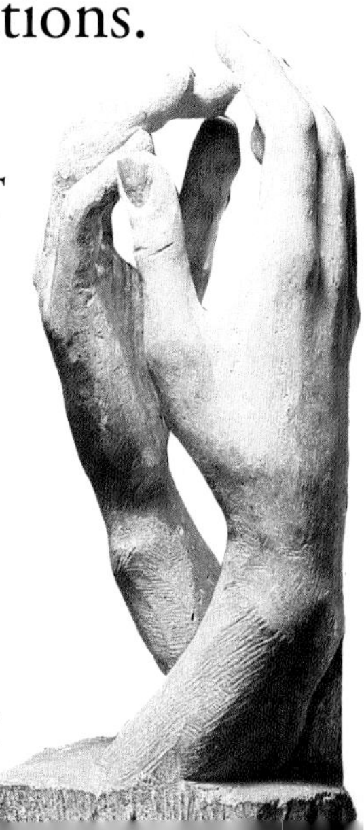

Retrospective in the Pavillon de l'Alma

On 1 June 1900 Georges Leygues, Minister for Education, opened the Rodin exhibition at the Pavillon de l'Alma. As this was his first retrospective to be held in France, Rodin wanted to make a strong impression. People who had come from all over the world to visit the International Exhibition were treated to a showing of 168 works in plaster, bronze and marble. Old works, new works, and even works in progress born from his constant experiments. On the walls were his drawings and seventy-one photographs by Eugène Druet. Finally, lectures explaining the artist's technique were given by Camille Mauclair, Charles Morice and Edmond Picard.

The exhibition at the Pavillon de l'Alma marked the end of his exhibitions abroad: Geneva, in 1896, with his

Rodin travelled the world with exhibitions of his work. In 1902, after a brief stay in Cologne and Dresden, he made a triumphant visit to Prague and Moravia, which is recorded in a series of postcards (below). An enthusiastic crowd met him at the station, and – just as they had in London – the students unhitched the horses from his carriage and pulled him all the way to his hotel.

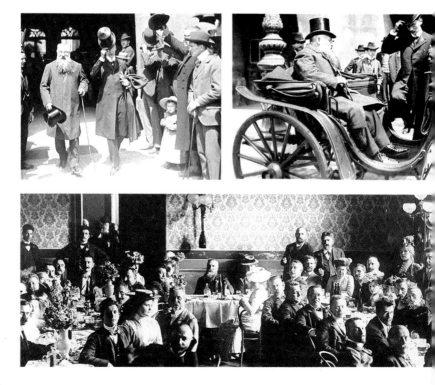

two old friends Pierre Puvis de Chavannes and Eugène Carrière; Brussels, in 1899; then Rotterdam, Amsterdam and The Hague, organized by Judith Cladel.

An enormous international success

Rodin had taken a great financial risk, as the enterprise would only be cost-effective if he succeeded in selling the works on display. When the exhibition closed, he wrote with relief to his friend Bigand-Kaire: 'I must also tell you that my exhibition is a fine success, both in terms of its "moral" outcome, and in terms of cash. I'll cover my costs. I've sold 200,000 francs' worth.... Almost all the museums have bought something. Philadelphia: *Thought*, Copenhagen, 80,000 francs for a whole room to myself in the museum, Hamburg, Dresden, Budapest, etc.... Not as much in entry fees as I expected but lots of sales.'

He was immensely popular with foreigners, and soon requests for exhibitions began to flood in, from Düsseldorf, Buenos Aires, Montreal, Tokyo, Berlin: Rodin's works began a world tour. The most successful exhibition of all was undoubtedly that held in Prague, and Rodin travelled there in 1902.

After the Paris retrospective Rodin had the Pavillon de l'Alma rebuilt in the grounds of the Villa des Brillants, where he reigned like a god. Meudon, where the monumental Buddha in the garden seemed to counsel wisdom, became a shrine to sculpture. Important foreigners and Frenchmen, artists, ambassadors and sovereigns all tried to obtain an invitation to the famous studio. In 1908 Rodin even received a visit from King Edward VII.

While organizing these exhibitions, Rodin was developing a theoretical

Rodin's works were designed to be seen from every angle, enabling the viewer to walk all round them, in the case of free-standing sculptures. The master was always particular about how his works were presented, and he had unusual ideas about how they should be displayed to best advantage. He would set them on columns over 2 m high, lending these 'fragile maquettes' the appearance of 'white birds sitting on their perches'.

discourse on his sculpture and on art in general. His
book *Les Cathédrales de France,* written with the help of
Charles Morice, was published to great acclaim in March
1914, a few months before the bombardment of
Rheims, which caused the sculptor great distress.

The rate of production never slackens

Rodin exploited the immense amount of work
he had produced in previous years by enlarging
and combining several of his earlier figures. He
worked on a variety of subjects, including the
strange monument to Puvis de Chavannes and
another to James Abbott McNeill Whistler,
whom he replaced as president of the International
Society of Sculptors, Painters and Gravers in London in
1903. He completed several long-term projects: the
Victor Hugo monument, for example, was unveiled in
1909. *The Thinker,* which had been submitted as early
as 1888, but on a small scale, was exhibited in a much
larger format at the Salon of 1904, where it gave rise
to an avalanche of criticism – as was the norm.

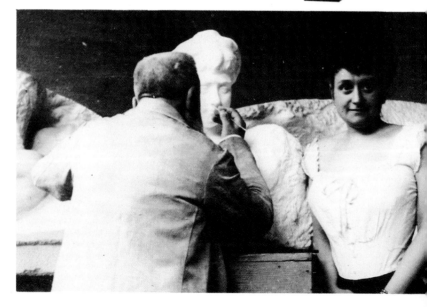

A subscription was launched to display the sculpture in one of the public squares of Paris; on the day of the unveiling, 21 April 1906, Mme Segond-Wéber declaimed passages from Hugo's *Stella* on the steps of the Panthéon.

Commissions poured in. According to some sources, as many as fifty assistants were working under the master's direction after 1900. The characteristic style of his late marble carvings – often described as unfinished, as the figure emerges from a block that seems to have been left in its raw state – ensured him immense success with foreign admirers. Among the creations of these last years are *The Hand of God*, *The Cathedral* and a fine series of small dancing figures embodying movement.

'A very knowledgeable man who pours souls into his marble statues, which quiver with life'

Above all, Rodin modelled portrait busts, particularly for rich English and Americans: Mrs Mary Hunter, a famous hostess of Edwardian London and great friend of the

painter John Singer Sargent, who introduced him to the Countess of Warwick, Miss Eve Fairfax, Victoria Sackville-West, the statesman George Wyndham, Joseph Pulitzer, the American press magnate, John Winchester de Kay, Mrs Kate Simpson, George Harriman, owner of the Union Pacific Railroad,

Rodin was captivated by the mysterious Cambodian dance tradition (below left, Rodin drawing one of the dancers who accompanied the king of Cambodia to the colonial exhibition held in Marseilles) and the dynamism of the Ballets Russes (opposite above, two figures of Nijinsky, in which the whole body has become a coiled spring of potential energy). Among the many busts he produced were those of the American art-collector Mrs Kate Simpson (opposite below) and the Japanese actress Hanako (above), whose intensity fascinated him.

Thomas F. Ryan, a financier and keen art collector, who established the first Rodin section at the Metropolitan Museum in New York, and many others.

But he also produced busts of his friends: Gustave Geffroy, Marcellin Berthelot, Anna de Noailles and Helene von Nostitz-Hindenburg. He was fascinated by the Japanese actress Hanako, introduced to him in 1908 by Loïe Fuller. He did fifty-three studies of her face.

He also modelled lively portraits of the last great love of his life, the Marquess – and bogus Duchess – Claire de Choiseul. Increasingly fatigued by his work, Rodin allowed himself to be taken in by this American-born schemer, the daughter of a well-known New York lawyer, whose only concern was to get her hands on his inheritance. Hundreds of drawings disappeared, until Rodin was eventually forced to accept that she just

Rodin and *The Hand of God* (below).

Among the portraits Rodin created at the height of his fame are those of many female admirers of the man and his work – both sincere and self-interested. From left to right: The *Duchess de Choiseul*, who for seven years was Rodin's 'evil genius', taking advantage of his old age and naïvety; the poet *Countess Anna de Noailles*, who was so disappointed by her bust that she initially refused to accept it; *Mrs Kate Simpson*, who played an important role in establishing contacts between the sculptor and the United States; and *Miss Eve Fairfax*, whose melancholy portrait may have been in Rilke's mind when he described these 'faces in which the smile never settles anywhere, but flickers over their features, with such misty softness that it seems it must vanish with every intake of breath; mysteriously half-closed lips and wide eyes that seem to gaze dreamily out at the radiant gleam of an eternally moonlit night, at a dream.'

wanted to profit from his work. He broke with her finally in 1911, to the great relief of those close to him, and returned to Rose Beuret in Meudon.

'He captures them effortlessly, with a rapid line'

Throughout his long career, Rodin never ceased drawing, but during the late 1890s he developed a new, more spontaneous style. He drew female nudes from the live model, employing a technique he explains as follows: 'It didn't come to me straight away. Part of me dared to do it, but I was afraid; then, gradually, in front of nature, as I began to understand better and to reject my prejudices more openly and to love her, I made up my mind, I tried....' He asked his models, whose names are mostly unknown to us, to behave as naturally as possible. 'Don't pretend to arrange your hair, do it.' The models were asked to wander around the studio while he followed them with his eyes, allowing his hand to run freely over the paper. 'I take the movements I observe straight from life, but I do not impose them.'

His drawing style is 'simplified in order to capture the essential'.

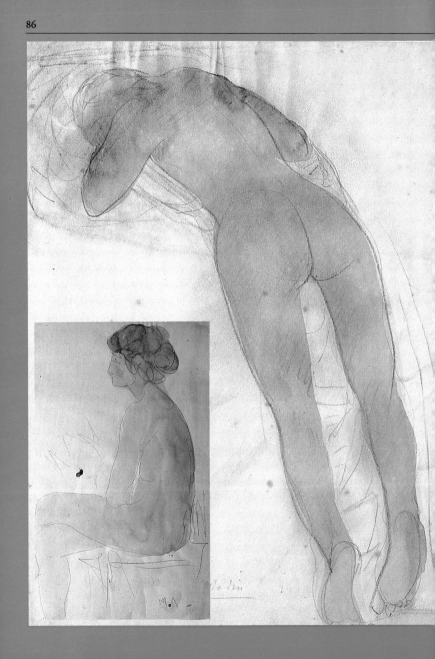

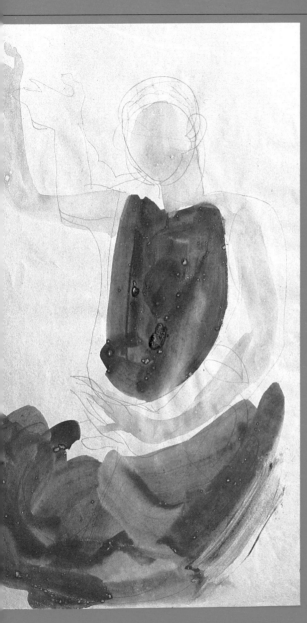

'The nude is a real religion with me'

From around 1900 Rodin began to fill pages with line drawings of women. Over fifteen hundred of these often provocative drawings – which include erotic nudes and lesbian couples – have been recorded.

The Symbolist poet and critic Arthur Symons wrote, 'In these astonishing drawings from the nude we see woman carried to a further point of simplicity than even in Degas: woman the animal; woman, in a strange sense, the idol. Not even the Japanese have simplified drawing to this illuminating scrawl.... These are the drawings of a sculptor, notes for sculpture, and thus indicating form as the sculptor sees it, with more brevity, in simple outline, than the painter. They speak a different language from the drawings of the painter, searching, as they do, for the points that catch the light along a line, for the curves that indicate contour tangibly. In looking at the drawings of a painter, one sees colour; here, in these short-hand notes of a sculptor, one's fingers seem actually to touch marble.'

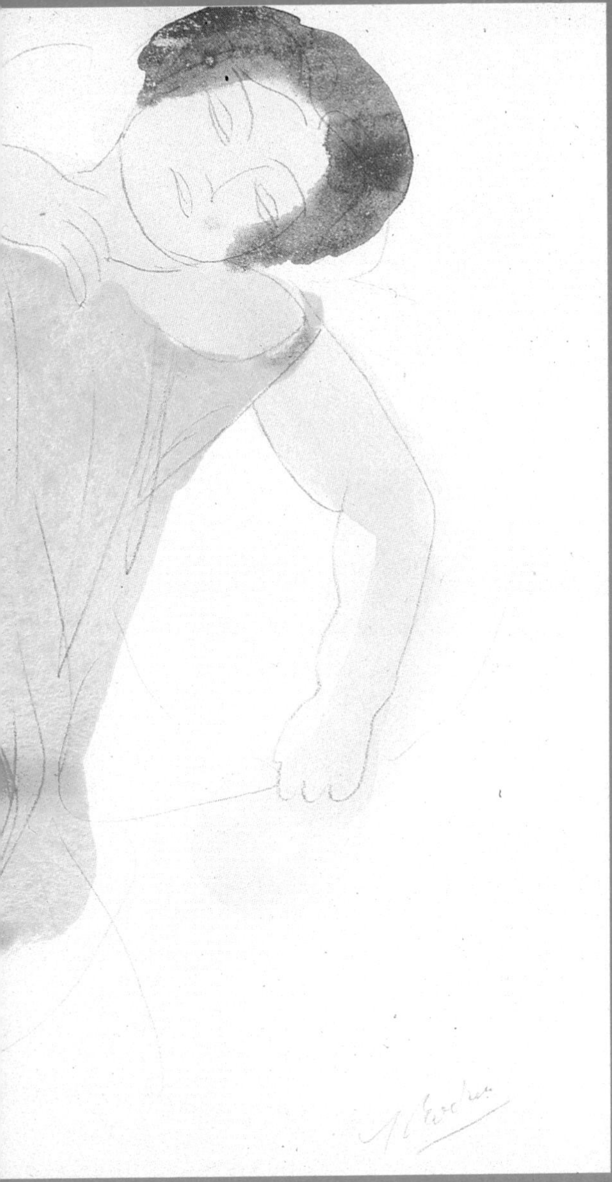

'These strange documents of the momentary'

"Don't you see that, for my work of modelling, I have not only to possess a complete *knowledge* of the human form, but also a deep *feeling* for every aspect of it? I have, as it were, to *incorporate* the lines of the human body, and they must become part of myself, deeply seated in my instincts. I must feel them at the end of my fingers. All this must flow naturally from my eye to my hand. Only then can I be certain that I understand. Now look! What is this drawing? Not once in describing the shape of that mass did I shift my eyes from the model. Why? Because I wanted to make sure that nothing evaded my grasp of it. Not a thought about the technical problem of representing it on paper could be allowed to arrest the flow of my feelings about it, from my eye to my hand. The moment I drop my eyes that flow stops. That is why my drawings are only my way of testing myself.... My object is to test to what extent my hands already feel what my eyes see."

Rodin
Quoted in Anthony
Ludovici
*Personal Reminiscences
of Auguste Rodin*, 1926

Jardin des
Suppliers

japonais

'Human flowers'

In the 1908 catalogue of Rodin's drawings Louis Vauxelles wrote, 'There is no question of interpreting the subject in these sketches, but of capturing life on the wing. The draughtsman-sculptor does not devise fantastic groups, Redonesque dreams. These disjointed dancers, distorted women, languid, damned, exhausted, fainting, their arms resting on pillows, are nothing less than life itself, captured and moulded. I say moulded, because these drawings comment on and anticipate marble or stone.' Rilke also emphasized their sculptural quality: 'A brush loaded with ochre, rapidly outlining the contours with changing accentuation, modelled the enclosed surface area with such incredible force that you might think you were looking at figures modelled in terracotta.'

Occasionally the sculptor would cut out the bodies he had drawn and attach them to a new background. Such techniques seemed 'eccentric and modern' to his contemporaries.

These works are not rapid notes, studies, or sketches. They represent the culmination of many years' continuous experience. Just as he isolated individual figures from his *Gates of Hell* or his other sculptural groups, so Rodin abstracted his nudes from all material associations, lending them an intrinsic significance.

Success: a string of secretaries

The exhibitions, commissions and visits took up a great deal of time and involved a considerable amount of paperwork. From the turn of the century Rodin employed secretaries to answer his post, file and translate the cuttings from French and foreign newspapers, and to take care of the many daily details with which an artist at the peak of his fame no longer has time to deal. A whole series of people took on this demanding role, including the poet Rainer Maria Rilke, who had been introduced to Rodin by his wife, the sculptor Clara Westhoff. Rodin did not allow his secretaries to use their own initiative, as Rilke discovered to his cost; he was dismissed for becoming too personally involved in some business correspondence with the painter William Rothenstein. Rodin later said: 'I quarrelled with Rilke through my impatience. He is a loyal friend.'

Rilke (above) thanked Rodin for the table he had given him at the Hôtel Biron (below), 'a table that will be the vast fertile plain on which I shall arrange my manuscripts like villages'.

The lord of art at the Hôtel Biron

In 1908 Rilke, who had made up with Rodin, wrote to the sculptor: 'My dear friend, you should come and see the beautiful building I moved into this morning. The three bays look out prodigiously over an abandoned garden, where from time to time you can see wild rabbits jumping through the trellises just like an old tapestry.'

The Hôtel Biron, which until the separation of Church and state had housed the religious community of Sacré-Coeur, was now for rent at a very low rate. Among the tenants, some were unknown, others were, or would be, famous: Jean Cocteau, Henri Matisse, Isadora Duncan and Rilke. '[Rodin rented] the whole of the ground floor and the first floor of the right wing, together with the square central room.... They were the kind of rooms he had always dreamt of in vain.... He wanted to have all manner of things displayed there, so he could come and look at them from time to time, and to gaze out at the garden through the imposing windows of this place where no one would ever think of looking for him.' Rilke was wrong; the Hôtel Biron soon became a highly valued place to visit.

Rodin's collections combined Egyptian bronzes and statuettes (above), Persian miniatures, Graeco-Roman busts and torsos; they were everywhere: in the sheds, in the gardens, in the studio, and even on the master's dining-room table.

'I bequeath all my works to the state'

After 1900 Rodin was awarded many honours. In 1903 he was made a commander of the Légion d'honneur, and Bourdelle organized a *fête champêtre* in the Bois de Vélizy to celebrate the occasion; many of Rodin's friends went to watch Isadora Duncan dance barefoot on the grass to violin music. He was awarded an honorary doctorate by the University of Jena in 1905, by the

University of Glasgow in 1906, and by the University of Oxford in 1907. Now that he was universally acclaimed, the sculptor only wished to establish a museum named after him.

When the tenants of the Hôtel Biron were ordered, by decree, to vacate the premises, Rodin was allowed extra time. He then proposed an exchange: 'I will bequeath to the state all my works, in plaster, marble, bronze and stone, together with my drawings, as well as the antiques that I have enjoyed collecting for the apprenticeship and training of artists and craftsmen. And I ask the state to keep all these collections in the Hôtel Biron, which will become the Rodin museum, allowing me to stay here for the rest of my life.' Rodin forgot to mention his archives, which were also to form part of the bequest, the press cuttings which he had been collecting since the early 1880s, the letters he had received, photographs of his works, and his library, containing many works dedicated to him.

His proposition was supported in the political sphere by Clemenceau, Paul Boncour and Aristide Briand. In artistic circles, Gustave Coquiot and Judith Cladel moved heaven and earth to help the plan succeed. A petition was organized and signed by Claude Debussy, Guillaume Apollinaire, Romain Rolland, Anatole France and Claude Monet. In 1912 the administrative council agreed that the artist should continue to enjoy use of the building for the rest of his days. War interrupted further negotiations. The minister Etienne Clémentel, a painter and amateur photographer, set the final and essential seal on the agreement, which was voted through in 1916.

The tomb at Meudon, dominated by *The Thinker*, in front of the façade of the Château d'Issy, where Rodin lies buried beside Rose Beuret.

Rodin had by then been severely weakened by a series of attacks. Several schemers continued to hover around him, and his close friends thought it would be wise for him to marry Rose Beuret. The wedding of the elderly lovers was performed on the 29 January 1917. Rose died on the 16 February, and Rodin on the 10 November. His funeral took place fourteen days later.

Well-known figures and friends attended the funeral. After the official speeches the journalist Séverine improvised an emotional farewell to the 'master'.

DOCUMENTS

Rodin and women

Assistants, admirers and evil genii, adored with tenderness or passion, lovingly modelled and drawn: women occupied a position of great importance in Rodin's life and work.

Rose Beuret

Anthony Ludovici, Rodin's secretary from 1906 to 1907, developed a certain sympathy for 'Madame' Rodin during his stay in Meudon.

I had, of course, ample opportunities of observing the relationship that existed between the great sculptor and the woman who was his closest companion during practically the whole of his adult life, and I have no hesitation in saying that it was an exceedingly happy one. Naturally, however, it had to be viewed from the proper standpoint, and due allowance made for the great disparity in cultivation and intellectual power between the two people. Regarded from the angle of a modern match between social equals, and with all the bias that modern feminism has fostered in favour of woman's so-called freedom, independence, or what-not, it might easily have struck one or two of our

Rodin and Rose Beuret, with their dogs, in the garden of the Villa des Brillants, Meudon.

A serious, almost severe face: Rose Beuret modelled by Rodin in 1890.

of before the meal, as the effort of bending over his feet and buttoning his boots, so soon after eating, disturbed her digestion. But never did I hear anything more serious than this, and even complaints of this kind were rare. She was an ingenuous and primitive creature, scarcely able to realize the exalted position her distinguished mate had conquered for himself among the artistic and cultured communities of the whole world; and perhaps always grieving a little secretly over the altered circumstances of the poor struggling sculptor who, having emerged from that obscurity which had once made him completely her possession, had become a public figure and institution, in whose active relations to the world outside she could not participate.

Anthony Ludovici
Personal Reminiscences of Auguste Rodin
1926

latter-day young women with horror. But this would have amounted to judging it according to a totally wrong standard, and one, moreover, to which both Rodin himself and Madame Rodin would have scorned to aspire. Madame Rodin who, very soon after my first appearance at the Villa des Brillants, paid me the honour of confiding in me concerning most of her difficulties and anxieties, hardly ever complained either about her mode of life or about the treatment she received at the hands of her lord and master; and her devotion seemed to set no limit to the services she cheerfully performed for him. Occasionally she might perhaps come to me, lamenting over the many harassing engagements and activities that sometimes conspired to ruffle Rodin's temper; or she might in a rare mood of revolt comment bitterly upon his thoughtlessness in asking her to put on his boots directly after luncheon, instead

Marcelle Tirel, Rodin's last secretary, records the following laconic exchange in her book, The Last Years of Rodin, *1925.*

A tawny cat, of which Madame Rodin was fond, jumped on to Rodin's knee and rubbed its head against his beard.

'Look,' said his wife, 'the cat is the same colour as your beard was when you were young. I wonder if he's as big a lady-killer as you were?'

'I behaved as a man does,' he retorted sharply.

'Red men', said Madame Rodin to me, 'are either very good or very bad.'

'I was often told that', remarked Rodin, 'when my hair was still red. Yet I never did any harm.'

'I don't suppose you remember,' muttered his wife.

Rodin left the room.

Camille Claudel: a love without compromise.

Camille Claudel

Camille Claudel was Rodin's lover and his equal. After the years of passion came the years of separation, but his 'pupil's' interests were always close to Rodin's heart.

[25 June 1892]

Monsieur Rodin

As I have nothing to do I am writing to you again. You cannot imagine how lovely it is here at L'Islette. Today I dined in the central room (which acts as a conservatory) from which you have a view of the garden on both sides. Madame Courcelles suggested (without my having said anything at all) that if you would like to, you could eat here from time to time, and even all the time (I think she is quite keen on the idea), and it is so pretty here!

I went for a walk in the countryside; everything has been mown and harvested, hay, wheat, oats, you can walk wherever you like and it's charming. If you are kind, and keep your promise, we could know paradise here. You can have whichever room you like to work in. I'm sure the old lady will be completely at our service.

She said that I might swim in the river, where her daughter and the maid go swimming quite safely. With your permission I will do so, because I enjoy it so much, and that would save me having to go the heated baths at Azay. Would you be very kind and buy me a little swimming costume – dark blue with white trimming, a two-piece with blouse and trousers (medium size), at the Louvre or the Bon Marché [department stores] (made of serge) or in Tours.

I sleep naked so I can imagine you are there too, but when I wake up it's never quite the same.

I kiss you.

Camille

Mind you're not unfaithful to me.

To Octave Mirbeau

[1895]

My dear Mirbeau

....As for Mademoiselle Claudel, who has as much talent as the Champ-de-Mars, she is almost totally ignored. You have a project for her, you said, in spite of the time of lies, you sacrificed yourself for her, for me, for your conviction. It is your good nature, Mirbeau, that creates the obstacles, your generosity that stands in your way. I don't know whether Mademoiselle Claudel will agree to visit you on the same day as me, we have not seen each other for two years and I haven't written to her. If I have to be there, Mademoiselle Claudel will decide. I feel a bit better, sometimes, when I am happy, but how cruel life is to us.

Chavannes should write a letter for the minister which some friends will sign, but at the moment I have little confidence in our success: in spite of everything everyone seems to think that Mademoiselle Claudel is my protégée, when in fact she is a misunderstood artist, she can boast of having had against her my sculptor friends as well as the others who always crippled me at the Ministry, because I was not familiar with its workings.

But don't let's give up hope, dear friend, because I am certain of her ultimate success, though the poor artist will be sad, more sad then, knowing life, regretting and crying perhaps over the fact that success has come too late, a victim of her artistic pride, which works honestly, regretting the strength she has spent in the battle to succeed and in attaining the fame that comes too late, leaving you illness in exchange.

My best wishes to you and to Madame Mirbeau.

Rodin
8 Chemin Scribe, Bellevue, Seine-et-Oise

My letter is too disheartened, don't let Mlle Claudel see it. I think Mlle Claudel's address is still 113 Bld d'Italie.

Hélène Wahl-Porgès

The painter Hélène Wahl-Porgès (left) accompanied Rodin on some of his travels. He started work on her bust in 1914.

[Meudon, 5 February 1896]

Dear Madame

I hope I have got over my worries as I am now able to work and sleep, I feel I am happy, or that I will be, because I feel young again, my head is full of enthusiasm, and the tyrannical passions seem definitely to have left me, I don't love women any less but in a different way, and, I might say, as my divine sisters, while still admiring the fine chiselling of their bodies and their heart. The Great Founder who made us all certainly patinated your sex better than he did ours....

Every morning I go to admire this new landscape, and the mists in this spot are very fine, the railways are constantly pouring out clouds of smoke, little mists in their own right, and you can feel infinity, and to imagine that you can paint all that, that you can do anything if you apply your talents to it.

Have you been working? And are you feeling better this week?

I send my sincere sympathy and express my respectful devotion.

A. Rodin

"The Great Founder ... certainly patinated your sex better than he did ours."

Eve Fairfax

Rodin was a great admirer of the beauty of English women. From 1902 to 1903 he executed a bust of Eve Fairfax (right), then aged thirty, daughter of Colonel Thomas Fairfax of the Grenadier Guards. Although the commission fell through, Rodin continued work on the portrait, the bronze of which is now in the Tate Gallery, London; three marble versions also exist.

18 July 1904

Highly honoured and dear Miss Fairfax and most honoured friend

I received your letter and am pleased that you are so kind and so devoted to your friends.

It is a female grace to be able to lend your strength, and so obligingly, to everything, to everyone.

You are the sun and the firmament in the supernatural order, and it is always astonishing how, in the great mass of conversations and writings that always concern you, concern woman, and among which there are many that are ignorant, against you, you always shine through like beneficent goddesses.

Even when you are not speaking, your gestures, your sober expressions, your movements (which are exactly as one might wish them to be) have an expressive quality that touches the artist's soul.

You know I would be happy to see you in Paris if you have the opportunity of coming here, and I am always with you through your bust, which is not yet completed, in marble. All best wishes, with respectful and grateful sympathy.

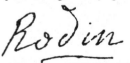

Gwen John

Following their first meeting in 1904, when she agreed to pose for Rodin, the English painter Gwen John began a passionate affair with the sculptor; they remained on intimate terms, if sporadically, for the best part of a decade, though the Duchess de Choiseul became her main rival for Rodin's affections. She wrote him nearly two thousand love letters – as many as three a day between 1906 and 1907. They are signed variously Mary, Marie or Your Obedient Little Model, but never Gwen.

[c. 1906]
Tuesday evening

Mon cher maître

I was so happy with you in the mist, and especially at the end you said

Gwen John posed for the *Muse* for the monument to Whistler, which was exhibited without arms at the 1908 Salon. Opposite: Eve Fairfax.

something – you know what I mean – what you said at the station. *Mon maître*, you are everything to me – my love, my wealth, my family. You are all I possess. I do not want this to annoy you, master, I would not wish to cause you a moment's irritation, not even when I am fired with jealousy or gripped by despair. I have more confidence in myself than you have in me. My love makes me docile, not naughty.

Your Mary

And in her journal she wrote:

There is something beautiful in me, not to be cut and left to die. This flower, with all my thoughts, however silly, belongs to Rodin. He will await its flowering.

Helene von Nostitz-Hindenburg

From 1901 to 1914 Rodin carried on a warm and voluminous correspondence with the German writer Helene von Nostitz-

Hindenburg (below), with whom he visited Italy. He made a bust of her in 1902.

After many years I again sit on the same shore that Rodin loved so well. A few sketches and drawings are around me, also two plaster torsos, half destroyed by unknowing hands. Like a wave of the sea, a female figure arises from the imprisonment of the clay out of which

"It made me profoundly happy to do your bust."

it grew. It is night, the moon gleams over the sea that speaks with sighs the eternal language of its longing. In such moments one feels strongly out of which source Rodin's forms emanated, for they fraternally greet all the voices of nature, and are her deepest expression. How nobly the torso of the man arises in front of the rosy oleander blossoms at morning, or the purple rays of the sunset, at night. Here, in this drawing, there are women entwined like plants, the scent of the forest around

them. For Rodin, earth and heaven were the scents that arose from woman, she is the flower that opens out of the night. In the garden of the Villa Margherita the white chalices of the *ipomoea* open at sunset with their overpowering aroma, only to die at the first ray of the sun. Rodin's female figures have something of this beauty, which knows nothing of the ugliness of fading. And even when he reproduces age in *The Old Helmet-maker's Wife* this degeneration has over it a glamour of eternal beauty.

Helene von Nostitz-Hindenburg
Dialogues with Rodin, 1931

Claire de Choiseul

For seven years, between 1904 and 1911, Claire de Choiseul exploited the old age and generous nature of the master. Marcelle Tirel witnessed her bad effect on Rodin, and eventually managed to reveal the 'Muse', as she styled her, in her true colours.

She wearied us with the recital of countless branches of the genealogical tree of the family into which she had married; their title was held from Louis XV one day, from Charles X the next. With the aid of an extra glass of whisky she would trace it, straight as the fall of a plummet, right down from Charlemagne.

To the rest of the world, however, it was of Rodin that she would boast, saying that he owed his glory to her.

'Rodin! I am Rodin!' she said.

Unhappily, her influence on him was most harmful; she interrupted his work, monopolized his attention, disorganized and weakened his powers, robbing French art of many a noble work. It must be acknowledged, however, that she worked for him in many ways as hard as any domestic. She washed his face, put on his boots, brushed his hair, dressed him, and put up with his ill-temper without complaint – and then revenged herself on his true friends and admirers. She practically succeeded in cutting him off from almost every acquaintance and keeping him as a close preserve.

She drugged his brain with her inept conversation ... and she used to reproach Rodin for taking possession of her, telling him that with her title she might have aspired to the highest....

I won't go into details of all the Muse's petty manoeuvres and intrigues. But one day I told Rodin the truth about her and gave him proofs. Poor Rodin!

"Madame is a proper little bacchante." Rodin with Claire de Choiseul, *c.* 1910.

He cried over his love like a fifteen-year-old schoolboy. We were in the big studio at Meudon. He sank back against the *Ugolino* statue shaking with sobs....

The forsaken Muse was wild with rage. She hurled threats at me. Then one day she appeared at the Hôtel Biron, swathed in black veils, flung herself at Rodin's feet and began a dramatic scene, wailing and sobbing. Rodin quietly rose, put down the drawing he was working on, called the servant, pointed to the crouching figure of the Muse, and said: 'Show Madame out!'

Marcelle Tirel
The Last Years of Rodin, 1925

Camille Claudel, sculptor

Destroyed by the contradictions of her destiny, Claudel is today being reassessed.

Until today critics have stressed the debt Camille Claudel owes to her master, Auguste Rodin. Even if we must accept this judgment overall, particularly in the case of works conceived before 1893, it is appropriate that we should begin to indicate its limitations.... Four main strands in fact dominate the artist's career: naturalism, anecdotalism, theatricality and tradition. These basic constituents are combined in certain compositions, but their relative importance varies according to the periods of Camille Claudel's life.

Realism would appear always to have been part of the sculptor's style; it is evident as early as 1882 in the *Bust of the Aged Helen*, and it is one of the essential characteristics of *L'Age mûr* and more commercially inspired works probably produced post-1900, such as the *Head of an Old Woman* in the Tissier collection. This tendency is clear in other creations, such as *The Waltz* and *Clotho*, but it is tempered, as in *L'Age mûr*, by an obviously personal element, which is evident in the web of *The Park* or in the compositional asymmetry of such autobiographical works as *The Waltz, L'Age mûr* or the design for *The Sin*.

From 1893 Camille Claudel begins to move in a new direction, which is made clear in the famous letter to Paul Claudel: studies from nature. The works belonging to this series are without doubt some of the most original ever produced by the artist. It is hard to think of a sculptural equivalent to *The Gossips*, the *Woman at her Toilet, The Wave* or *Intimacy*. In these groups Camille Claudel reveals extraordinary dexterity in miniaturizing scenes created in materials as

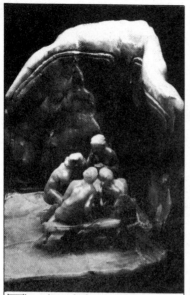

The realism of *The Waltz* (left), presented to the Salon in 1893, and the intimacy of *The Gossips*, 1897.

difficult to carve as onyx, for example. She also reveals a pronounced concern for originality, in relation to her master. She expresses this in a letter to her brother: 'You can see that it isn't Rodin any more, not in any way at all.'

From her early busts, and especially in *My Brother* of 1886, Camille Claudel underlines her own presence as artist through her concern for theatricality, by 'historicizing' her subjects. Thus, Paul Claudel is shown as a young Roman, Louise de Massary as a young girl under the Ancien Régime, and, a few years later, the Comte de Maigret is dressed as an aristocrat from the reign of Henri II. In parallel with this series, Camille Claudel produced more traditional commissioned portraits, such as that of her brother-in-law Ferdinand de Massary and of the painter Léon Lhermitte, which are marked primarily by a desire for physical resemblance.

From 1897, without rejecting the characteristics of her early works completely, Camille Claudel seems to have abandoned expressionism in favour of a more traditional style. Works such as *Perseus and the Gorgon* indicate, indeed, a surprising classicism, which marks the new direction taken at the time of her final break with Rodin. It would appear that, once more, this new choice – which seems to have been made by the artist in 1895, since she was already working on the *Hamadryad* at this time – was determined by the desire to distinguish her own style clearly from that of her master. In 1906 *The Wounded Niobid* was also created with an evident interest in full and harmonious forms, which characterize the works of this period. Nevertheless, the pose conferred on the figure by the artist recalls the asymmetrical compositions that had characterized the autobiographically inspired groups.

Finally, in 1905, the *Bust of Paul Claudel Aged 37* foreshadows the development of 20th-century French portrait sculpture and demands comparison with the style of [Robert] Wlérick, for example.... An epic, intoxicating, indeed tragic spirit animates the sculptures of an artist whom, through this exhibition, we have tried to rediscover, and whom we would wish to see restored to her rightfully important position in the history of sculpture at the turn of the century.

Bruno Gaudichon
Curator of the Musée de Poitiers
Camille Claudel catalogue, 1984

Rodin and writers

Rodin was fascinated by Dante, Balzac, Baudelaire and Hugo. But he also moved in the literary circles of his own age, who recognized his genius and supported him in their writings.

Rilke stressed the importance of literature in Rodin's work, and in particular the works of Dante and Baudelaire.

In books ... he found many ideas that gave him encouragement. He read Dante's *Divine Comedy* for the first time, and it came as a revelation to him. The suffering bodies of an earlier generation passed before him. He saw a century with all its outer garments stripped away; he witnessed the poet's great and eternal judgment on his own age....

From Dante he came to Baudelaire.... In this poet's verses there were prominent passages that appeared to have been not written, but moulded; words and phrases that had melted under the poet's glowing touch; lines that resembled reliefs, and sonnets that supported the weight of a developing thought like columns with elaborately decorated capitals. He sensed that this poetic art, at its limits, bordered on the outer limits of another art, and that it reached out towards this other art. He sensed in Baudelaire the artist who had been his precursor, who had sought bodies, in which life is greater, more cruel and more restless, rather than misleading faces.

Once he had read the works of these two poets, he was never parted from them again. His thoughts were inspired by them and then returned to them again: whenever his art was about to find expression in form, whenever the life he saw before him seemed lacking in meaning. Rodin lived in the works of the poets and nourished himself with the past. Later, when he attained those realms as a creator in his own right, their figures rose before him like memories of his own past, painful, real, and entered his work as if they were returning home.

Rainer Maria Rilke
Rodin, 1902

LES FLEURS DU MAL   47

Les poètes devant mes grandes attitudes,
Qu'on dirait que j'emprunte aux plus fiers monuments,
Consumeront leurs jours en d'austères études ;

Car j'ai pour fasciner ces dociles amants
De purs miroirs qui font les étoiles plus belles :
Mes yeux, mes larges yeux aux clartés éternelles !

In 1882 Rodin sculpted *I am Beautiful* and had the words of Baudelaire's poem engraved on the base. On Paul Gallimard's request he re-used his studies to illustrate *Les Fleurs du Mal*.

William Ernest Henley (1849–1903)

It was in 1881, during his first visit to London, that Rodin was first introduced to the poet and critic Henley, by the engraver Alphonse Legros. Henley, the publisher of Rudyard Kipling, H. G. Wells, Henry James and Robert Louis Stevenson (he is even said to have inspired the character of Long John Silver in Treasure Island *!), quickly recognized the sculptor's talent and used his position as editor of the* Magazine of Art *to help establish Rodin's reputation in England. In November 1881 he wrote to Rodin: 'Let me know what you are doing, and I shall then inform my readers – with or without blowing trumpets, as you please.' They carried on a lively correspondence until 1903.*

In 1884 Rodin executed a bust of Henley: 'The bust is thought to be very fine and very like me, but somewhat too lean and too much the dreamer, not quite so flamboyant and English as the poor sitter.' A cast of the bust was installed in the crypt of St Paul's Cathedral in London in 1907, under Rodin's direction. The sculptor also dedicated a plaster model of the Metamorphoses of Ovid, *now in the Tate Gallery, London, 'To the poet W. E. Henley, his old friend A. Rodin'.*

Here is sculpture in its essence.... You may read into it as much literature as you please, or as you can; but the interpolation is not Rodin's, but your own.... It is not literature in relief, nor literature in the round; it is sculpture pure and simple.... Passion is with him wholly a matter of form and surface and line, and exists not apart from these.... He is our Michelangelo.

W. E. Henley
Quoted in Camille Mauclair
Auguste Rodin, 1905

Octave Mirbeau (1850–1917)

The critic and novelist Mirbeau was one of the very first writers to defend Rodin. The sculptor had stayed with him for a fortnight on one occasion and for a whole month on another. Mirbeau confided to one of the Goncourt brothers (*Journal*, Wednesday 3 July 1889), that 'when this silent man comes face to face with nature he becomes eloquent, a speaker full of interest, and who knows a great many things, which he has taught himself, and which cover anything from theogonies to the techniques of every profession.'

There are several indications of their long friendship. First, the 192 letters

preserved by the Musée Rodin; then the terracotta bust Rodin made of his friend in 1889; the preface Mirbeau wrote in

1897 for an edition of Rodin's collected drawings; and finally the illustrations Rodin provided for a special edition of Mirbeau's novel *Le Jardin des Supplices* in 1899.

Mirbeau is said to have preferred the sculptor's drawings to his sculptures, and indeed it was Mirbeau and his work that lay at the root of Rodin's late style of drawing, in which he observed the model very freely. Mirbeau was also an enlightened art lover, and it was he who advised Rodin to purchase Vincent van Gogh's portrait of *Père Tanguy*.

Anna de Noailles (1876–1933)

It was in 1906 that Rodin did the poetess 'the supreme honour of creating a face that can never perish'. In La Vie parisienne *(24 August 1912) she described how it was more like posing for a film-maker than for a sculptor. Rodin was careful never to have a fixed, immobile model in front of him; he*

preferred natural ease and a freedom of movement.

Marcelle Tirel describes the Countess de Noailles' reaction to her bust:

She was far from pleased with it, and told him so. He was extremely angry. I advised him to write to her himself. He did so. He began by expressing his regret at not having satisfied her, then he added, naïvely, that her bust was among the works chosen by the Metropolitan Museum of New York. He asked the illustrious lady for permission to enter it in the catalogue as a Minerva or an archaic Venus.

The next day in came the lady and expressed her disappointment to Rodin himself – not in poetry, but hard emphatic prose.

'I've no luck with women,' Rodin said to me, 'even when they are poetesses.'

Anna de Noailles did not bear a grudge against Rodin, however, and in thanking her for some poems she had sent him, Rodin wrote, 'You say the simplest things in the world, and you are the first to have expressed them; you reveal to us a hidden treasure, as if you had discovered the radium that has lain sleeping for centuries under our very noses.'

Rainer Maria Rilke (1875–1926)

Rilke called Rodin the 'inexhaustible master'. He had learnt to appreciate him through the sculptor Clara Westhoff, whom he married in 1901. On 2 September 1902 Rilke met Rodin for the first time. By 1903 he had published a book about him, and in September 1905 he accepted the sculptor's invitation to stay at Meudon.

He received me, but it means nothing if I say cordially; in the way a beloved place receives one, to which one returns by

Rilke, Beuret, Rodin at Meudon, *c.* 1906.

beautiful shoulders and cheeks, and from afar reads on their lips the inexpressible. And with him everything is in blossom. How all that has grown! And how one understands and loves all the new as that which had to come, the most necessary, most inward, decreed, destiny! He moves like a star. He is beyond all measure.

Letter to Clara Rilke
15 September 1905

As the result of a misunderstanding between the two men, they separated in May 1906. The artist realized a year later that it was up to him to forget his grievances, and he was quick to accept when Rilke invited him to see the place where he was now living, at 77 Rue de Varenne – the Hôtel Biron and future Musée Rodin.

paths that have become more overgrown: a spring that, while one was away, has sung and lived and mirrored, day and night – a grove above which birds of passage have flown back and forth, spreading shadows over its tracery – a path lined with roses that hasn't ceased leading to those remote places; and like a big dog he greeted me, recognizing me with exploring eyes, contented and quiet; and like an eastern god enthroned, moved only within his sublime repose and pleasure and with the smile of a woman and a child's grasping gesture. And led me about. Now things are well with him; much more world has grown about him; he has built several little houses from the museum downward on the garden slope. And everything, houses, passages, and studios and gardens: everything is full of the most wonderful antiquities that associate with his dear things as with relatives, the only ones they have, happy, when the thousand eyes in their bodies open, not to be looking out into an unfamiliar world. And he is happy, and strokes their

Henri Rochefort (1830–1913)

The celebrated and flamboyant pamphleteer was editor of *L'Intransigeant* when he first met Rodin through Edmond Bazire. In 1884 he posed, somewhat impatiently, for a bust by Rodin. According to Rochefort, the sculptor spent an hour applying a ball of clay to the end of his nose and forehead, then another hour removing it again; it was the bust of Penelope, he declared. Nevertheless, allowance must be made for the sitter's irascible and impatient character; Rodin complained that he 'could not keep still for a single instant'. Rochefort charmed Rodin with his wit, and they discovered a mutual interest in antiques. However, the journalist did not always approve of Rodin's art. He called the *Balzac* a 'snowman', and failed to appreciate the fine qualities of his own bust, enlarged in 1897, which Mirbeau described as the 'fine head of a Roman Caesar'. The bust bears a strong resemblance to Edouard Manet's 1881 portrait of Rochefort.

"The adventurous bust of Henri Rochefort."

Arthur Symons (1865–1945)

The English Symbolist poet and critic Arthur Symons, publisher of Aubrey Beardsley and Joseph Conrad, was a leading figure in the Decadent movement.

Every figure that Rodin has created is in the act of striving towards something: a passion, an idea, a state of being, quiescence itself. His *Gates of Hell* is a headlong flight and falling, in which all the agonies of a place of torment, which is Baudelaire's rather than Dante's, swarm in actual movement. *Femmes damnées* lean upward and downward out of hollow caves and mountainous crags, they cling to the edge of the world, off which their feet slip, they embrace blindly over a precipice, they roll together into bottomless pits of descent. Arms wave in appeal, and clasp shuddering bodies in an extremity of despair. And all this sorrowful and tortured flesh is consumed with desire, with the hurrying fever of those who have only a short time in which to enjoy the fruits of desire. They live only with a life of desire, and that obsession has carried them beyond the wholesome bounds of nature, into the violence of a perversity which is at times almost insane....

In Rodin's sculpture, clay or marble, that something powerful of which he speaks has ended in a palpitating grace, as of living flesh. He feels, he translates, sensation for sensation, the voluptuous soft cool warmth of the flesh, the daintiness of the skeleton, indicated under its smooth covering; all that is exquisite in the structure of bone and muscle, in the force of man and the suppleness of woman. His hand seems to press most caressingly about the shoulder-blades and the hollows of the loins. The delicate ridge and furrow of the backbone draw his hand to mould them into new shapes and motions of beauty. His hand follows the loins where they swell into ampler outlines: the back, from neck to croup, lies quivering, in all the beauty of life itself.

Arthur Symons
Fortnightly Review, June 1902

George Bernard Shaw (1856–1950)

In the year 1906 it was proposed to furnish the world with an authentic portrait-bust of me before I had left the prime of life too far behind. The question then arose: could Rodin be induced to undertake the work? On no other condition would I sit, because it was clear to me that Rodin was not only the greatest sculptor then living, but the greatest sculptor of his epoch: one of those extraordinary persons who, like

George Bernard Shaw takes up the pose of *The Thinker*.

Michelangelo, or Phidias, or Praxiteles, dominate whole ages as fashionable favourites dominate a single London season. I saw, therefore, that any man who, being a contemporary of Rodin, deliberately allowed his bust to be made by anyone else, must go down to posterity (if he went down at all) as a stupendous nincompoop.

George Bernard Shaw
The Nation, 9 November 1912

On 26 April 1906 Rilke wrote to the English artist William Rothenstein: 'Shaw's bust is already going ahead wonderfully, and it is full of life and character, and this of course is possible only because Mr Shaw is such an unusual subject and he poses with that same vital sincerity which makes him such an incomparable writer.'

Yesterday, at the third sitting, he placed Shaw in a cunning little child's armchair, all of which caused this ironic and not uncongenial scoffer immense amusement, and cut off the head of the bust with a wire. (Shaw, whom the bust already resembled in a supercilious sort of way, witnessed this decapitation with indescribable joy.) Rodin then began working with the head reclining on two wedge-shaped supports, viewing it from above from roughly the same angle as the model sitting low down at arm's-length from him. Then the head was set upright again, and the work now continues in the same fashion. To begin with Shaw stood, often quite close to the stand, so that he was a little higher than the bust. But now he sits right next to it, at exactly the same height as the clay model and parallel with it. At some distance away a dark curtain has been hung so that the profiles always stand out clearly. The Master works rapidly, compressing hours into minutes, it seems to me, executing stroke after stroke at very short intervals, during which he assimilates tremendously, filling himself with form. You feel somehow that his lightning, hawklike swoops only fashion one of the many faces that come streaming into him, and you only grasp his working technique from memory, long after the sitting is over.

Rainer Maria Rilke
Letter to Clara, 19 April 1906

To create *Balzac* (top left) and *Victor Hugo* (top right), Rodin tried to absorb the writers' spirit by returning to the places where they had lived, in the Touraine and on Guernsey, respectively. Above: Several studies for the head of *Balzac*.

Rodin and photography

Over seven thousand photographs, many taken under the watchful eye of the sculptor, build up a veritable anthology of Rodin's sculpted work. During his lifetime they contributed greatly to his international success.

Rodin, *Victor Hugo* and *The Thinker*: a montage photographed by the American Edward Steichen in 1906.

Nineteenth-century sculptors did not generally consider the camera as a potential rival. There is no trace, in the annals of sculpture, of a reaction analogous to that of contemporary painters, who, in 1862, protested against the acceptance of photography into art in general, and into their art in particular.

The reason for this was that the sculptor's work, more than that of the painter, involved the use of instruments and the obligatory intervention of a workforce (assistants, founders) who had always made the business of producing multiple copies of a work of art quite familiar to the sculptor. In addition, photography offered certain technical possibilities that were comparable to those of sculpture: for example, like the sculptor's plaster model, the photographic image could be mechanically copied, enlarged or reduced.... These operations, which are inherent to both sculpture and photography, hinted at an 'industrial' character that tended to repel the artistic community, who were convinced, with Baudelaire, that the 'true art lover never confuses art with industry'.

Artists in every field have nonetheless discovered that the techniques of

photography offer an ideal opportunity for making their works more widely known, an economical way of obtaining permanent, cheap models to study, and also a valuable means of enriching the documentary material they amass on a particular theme or subject, before transforming it into a work of art....

It is not simply because he made use of photography that Rodin can be seen as a precursor in the medium; it is his frequent and varied use of the technique that places him unquestionably on the level of an innovator. In complete contradiction to his practice, he rarely commented on photography except in a pejorative tone. Nevertheless, through his contacts with the numerous photographers with whom he socialized, Rodin's attitude gradually changed. In the 1880s, his most creative period in terms of sculpture, he integrated the camera effortlessly into his studio, treating it as just another of the many tools that were already to be found there.

From 1896, the date of the exhibition held in Geneva, at which twenty-eight photographs were shown, illustrating, for the most part, sculptures that were not on display to the public, Rodin understood the full value of an image that could be multiplied *ad infinitum* and at minimal cost. Photographs would enable him to substantiate the discourse he was developing on his work.... Rodin then began to employ a series of photographers, whom he asked to produce – more or less under his guidance – a full photographic record of his works. The results were essentially documentary in the case of [Jacques-Ernest] Bulloz' images, progressing towards an increasingly marked artistic exploration in the case of [Eugène] Druet, and culminating in the work of [Stephen] Haweis and [Henry] Coles, and that of the American [Edward] Steichen.

Hélène Pinet
Rodin, Sculptor, and the Photographers of His Age, 1985

Steichen's famous portrait of Rodin (below left) apparently took a whole year to produce, and he made studies of several of Rodin's works, including the Balzac, *which he photographed by moonlight. Rodin was most impressed with the results: 'The prints seemed to give him more pleasure than anything I had ever done,' Steichen recalled. 'He said, "You will make the world understand my* Balzac *through these pictures. They are like Christ walking in the desert." '*

I believe that photography can create works of art, but hitherto it has been extraordinarily bourgeois and babbling. No one ever suspected what could be got out of it; one doesn't even know today what to expect from a process which permits of such profound sentiment, and such thorough interpretation of the model, as has been realized in the hands of Steichen. I consider Steichen a very great artist and the leading, the greatest photographer of the time. Before him nothing conclusive had been achieved. It is a matter of absolute indifference to me whether the photographer does, or does not, distort reality. I do not know to what degree Steichen interprets, and I do not see any harm whatever, or why it matters, what means he uses to achieve his results. I care only for the result, which, however, must always remain clearly a photograph. It will always remain interesting when it is the work of an artist.

Rodin
Camera Work, October 1908

Open house at the master's famous studios

Friends, artists and politicians all visited the sculptor in his studio. Overcoming his usual shyness, Rodin took pleasure in explaining his art to them.

Working space, living space

Space is a basic necessity for any sculptor. During his lifetime Rodin had about twenty different studios, where he worked and stored his sculptures; he sometimes occupied up to six at any one time.

1863–4: 96 Rue Lebrun, Paris, 13th arrondissement
1865: 5 Rue Hermel, Paris, 18th
1864–71: Blvd de Clichy, Paris, 9th
1871: 36 Rue du Pont-Neuf, Brussels
1872–7: 111 Rue Sans-Souci, Ixelles (suburb of Brussels)
1877–82: 268 Rue Saint-Jacques, Paris, 5th
1877–86: 36 Rue des Fourneaux, Paris, 15th
1880–1917: Dépôt des Marbres, 182 Rue de l'Université, Paris, 7th
1885: 17 Rue Saint-Egérie, Paris, 15th
1886–7: 10 Rue Poinsot, Paris, 14th
1885–90: 117 Blvd de Vaugirard, Paris, 15th
1887–95: 17 Rue du Faubourg-Saint-Jacques, Paris, 14th
1888–1902: 113 Blvd d'Italie, Paris, 13th (with Camille Claudel)
1890–8: La Folie-Neubourg, Rue du Chant-de-l'Alouette, Paris, 13th (with Claudel)
1896–1917: Villa des Brillants, Rue Paul-Bert, Meudon
1898–1917: 14 Rue des Vignes, Meudon
1904–17: 10 Rue de l'Orphelinat, Meudon
1908–17: 1 Rue du Château, Issy-les-Moulineaux
1908–17: Hôtel Biron, 77 Rue de Varenne, Paris, 7th

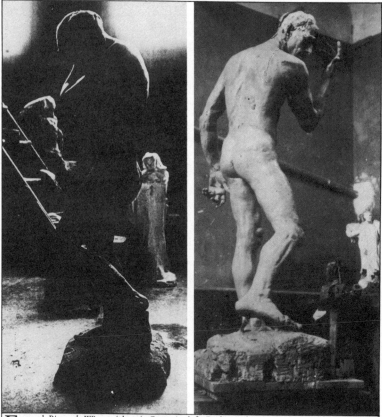

E*ve* and *Pierre de Wissant* (above). Opposite left: Rodin at the Dépôt des Marbres with *Thought* in the background, and (opposite right) the key to his studio.

117 Boulevard de Vaugirard

It was here, in one of Rodin's main studios, that he created The Burghers of Calais.

We found him in his studio on the Boulevard de Vaugirard, an ordinary sculptor's studio with its walls splashed with plaster, a wretched little cast-iron stove, the damp chill that rose from all the large compositions in wet clay wrapped in cloths, and a litter of heads, arms, and legs in the midst of which two emaciated cats looked like fantastic griffins. There was a model there, stripped to the waist, who looked like a stevedore. Rodin rotated the model-stands that carried the life-size clay figures of his six *Burghers of Calais*, which are modelled with forceful realism, and with those superb hollows in the human flesh that Barye used to create in the flanks of his animals. He showed us a powerful sketch of a naked woman, an Italian, a short, wiry creature, a panther, as he put it, which he said regretfully he would never be able to finish, as one of his pupils, a Russian, had fallen in love with her and married her.

From his Boulevard de Vaugirard studio Rodin took us to his studio near the Ecole Militaire [Dépôt des Marbres] to see the famous doorway destined for the future Palace of the Decorative Arts. The two enormous panels are covered with a tangled, confusing jumble, something like a bank of madrepore coral. Then, after a few seconds, the eye begins to distinguish among what appeared at first sight to be a coral reef, protrusions and hollows, the projections and cavities of a whole world of delightful little figures, moving, so to speak, in such a way that Rodin's sculpture seems to borrow something of the epic animation of Michelangelo's *Last Judgment*, a quality reminiscent of certain tumultuous crowd scenes in the paintings of Delacroix – all this with an unequalled relief, which only Dalou and he have ever dared to attempt.

The Boulevard de Vaugirard studio contains a wholly realistic humanity; the studio of the Ile des Cygnes [Dépôt des Marbres] is, as it were, the home of a poetic humanity, drawn from Dante.

> Jules and Edmond Goncourt
> Entry for Saturday 17 April 1886
> *Journal*, 1892

The Dépôt des Marbres

Rodin used this atelier from 1880, while working on The Gates of Hell.

It is an *atelier* in the true sense of the word, in the sense of a workshop, a place of labour, a room that exists only to facilitate the work that is carried out there. There are no soft furnishings anywhere, no knick-knacks; a few paintings by friends are hidden behind sheets to protect them from the plaster dust. The decoration consists entirely of the clay models wrapped in their damp cloths, unformed greyish masses that contain a dream, the maquettes of future works, works in preparation, the works of today.

You do not need to look around you for long to realize that you are in the presence of a worker who is haunted by his own thoughts, who is virtually indifferent to the outside world, who has no need of the excitements of everyday life beyond his clay and his modelling stand.

It is as if the very air were impregnated with work, with a whole lifetime's work, relentless, ruthless work, work that has never drawn back from any challenge

"This vast, bright hall, where all these dazzling white statues seem to gaze out at you from the many high glass doors, like fauna in an aquarium."

and has never relaxed in the satisfaction of having reached a point of completion.

Edouard Rod
'L'Atelier de M. Rodin'
in *La Gazette des Beaux-arts*, May 1898

In one corner were half-a-dozen Italian models, engaged to come around in case the master should want them. In another part a couple of street musicians, a man with a harp and a fiddler, were playing airs of street songs, while across the studio Rodin sat watching every movement. He wanted to do some studies of musicians. Finally, in still another part of the studio, several students – rather say apprentices – were

working away for dear life. Some were pointing up a big group of the master's; one was working on a study of her own. In the whole place was breathed the atmosphere of work – work.

Phillip Hale
The Boston Commonwealth, 1895

The studio at Meudon

This was installed in the pavilion in which Rodin had held his 1900 retrospective exhibition, which was reconstructed in the garden of the Villa des Brillants.

The villa, which he described as *un petit château Louis XIII*, is not attractive. It has

a three-window façade, made of red and
yellowish brick, with a steeply sloping
grey roof and tall chimneys. Below it lies
the 'picturesque' disorder of the Val
Fleury, a narrow valley full of shabby
houses that resemble those in Italian
vineyards.... You cross a bridge, then
walk along another stretch of road past a
small inn, which also has an Italian look
about it. The entrance is on the left. First
there is a long avenue of chestnut trees,
strewn with coarse gravel. Then you
come to a small wooden, latticed door.
A second little latticed door. Then you
round the corner of the small red-yellow
house and stand – as if before a miracle
– before a garden full of stone and plaster
figures. His large pavilion, the one that
was in the exhibition at the Pont de
l'Alma, has been transported into his
garden, which it seems to fill completely,
along with several other studios where
there are stonemasons and where he
himself works. There are also additional
rooms for firing clay and for every kind
of manual work. The effect of this vast,
bright hall, where all these dazzling white
statues seem to gaze out at you from the
many high glass doors, like fauna in an
aquarium, is extremely powerful and
strange. It makes a great, an immense
impression.... Even before you enter,
you can feel that these hundreds of lives
are in fact only one life – the vibrations
of a single force and a single will. There is
so much there ... everything, everything.
The marble carving of *The Prayer*, and
plaster casts of almost everything. The
products of an entire century, you might
say, an army of work. There are huge
glass showcases full of superb fragments
from *The Gates of Hell*. It defies
description. There it all lies, nothing but
fragments, side by side, for metre upon
metre. Nude figures the size of my hand,
other larger ones, but only pieces,

"Each represents a bit of love, devotion,
generosity and searching."

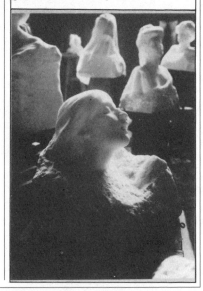

scarcely one that is whole: often only a piece of arm, part of a leg, which happen to be lying side by side, and nearby, the trunk that belongs to them. Elsewhere, the torso of one figure with the head of another pressed against it, and the arm of a third ... as if some unspeakable tempest, some unprecedented cataclysm had befallen his works. Yet the more closely you look, the more deeply you feel that this would all be less complete if the individual figures were themselves complete.

Each fragment of this debris possesses such an exceptional and striking unity, each one is so possible by itself, and requires so little to be completed, that one forgets that these are only parts, indeed often parts belonging to different bodies, which cling so passionately together here. One suddenly realizes that to see the body as a whole is really the role of the scholar, and that the artist's job is rather to use these elements to create new relationships, new unities, greater, more logical, more eternal.... And this inexhaustible richness, this infinite, continual invention, this presence, this purity, and vehemence of expression, this youthfulness, this gift of having always something more and something better to say, is without parallel in human history.

Then there are more tables, more turntables, chests covered with tiny figures – made of golden brown and ochre yellow baked clay. Arms no larger than my little finger, but so full of life that they make your heart beat faster. Hands that would cover a ten-pfennig piece, and yet filled with such an abundance of wisdom, so precisely defined, without the least trace of preciousness, that you might think they had been enlarged out of all proportion by a giant: thus this man creates them,

on his own scale. He is so great. Even if he makes them quite small, as small as he can, they are still greater than people.... There are hundreds and hundreds of them there, not one of which is like any other, and each one is a sensation, each represents a bit of love, devotion, generosity, and searching.

Rainer Maria Rilke
Letter to Clara, 2 September 1902

A visit from an English painter

Rodin first met William Rothenstein in March 1894. The two soon became friends and met frequently in London, Paris and Meudon. As director of the Carfax Gallery in London, Rothenstein was helpful in promoting the sculptor's work in England. Here Rothenstein describes his first meeting with the great sculptor.

Legros of course went to visit Rodin; Rodin was his closest friend; and I received an unexpected welcome when I found myself, with Legros, at the studio in the Rue de l'Université. I had long revered Rodin from afar: I had seen him once at the *vernissage* of the Salon, and admired his magnificent head; now I was face to face with the man, and his works.

I had heard of his greatest work, on which he had been engaged for years, *Les Portes d'Enfer* [*The Gates of Hell*]. If I was a little disappointed when I saw the actual work, I did not confess it to myself: a colossal conception, I had thought, and I imagined a grandiose result. I was more impressed by the *Victor Hugo* group; the figure of *Victor Hugo*, nude, and with outstretched arm, was grand and arresting; equally impressive were the attendant Fates. There were other figures and busts on which Bourdelle, then acting as Rodin's assistant was busy. All of these I saw, as I saw Rodin himself, through a prism of hero-worship. Every word Rodin said seemed pregnant with meaning, as I watched him working the clay with his powerful hands. When I drew him I felt I had never seen a grander head. I noticed how strongly the nose was set in the face, how ample its width between the brows, how bold the junction of the forehead with the nose. The eye was small and clear in colour, with a single sweeping crease from the corner of each and over the cheek bone, and the hair grew strongly on his head, like the hair of a horse's mane, like the crest of a Grecian helmet; and again I noticed the powerful hands, with the great thumbs, square-nailed. I think Legros must have told Rodin that I had been helpful to him; for Rodin was more than friendly, and almost embarrassed me by his attention. I must come and stay with him at Meudon, he said, before returning to London. At his house at Meudon I was able to study Rodin's work at my ease. Besides many now well-known pieces, he showed me a cupboard full of *maquettes*, exquisitely modelled. He would take two or three of these and group them together, first in one way and then in another. They gave him ideas for his compositions, he said....

In the evenings we walked in his garden, and looked down on the Seine and on the distant panorama of Paris, bathed in the warm glow of the evening mist. During a walk, Rodin embarrassed me by remarking: 'People say I think too much about women.' I was going to answer with conventional sympathy – 'but how absurd!' – when Rodin, after a moment's reflection, added, 'Yet, after all, what else is there more important to think about?'

I was eager to get people in England to realize Rodin's genius; Henley and Sargent would support efforts on his behalf. I was, in fact, able to be of some service to Rodin; and I call to mind, how, a year or two later, he said: 'I want to do something for you in return; I have engaged the most beautiful model in Paris; you shall come and draw her.' What a charming acknowledgment from an old artist to a young one, I thought. The model was indeed beautiful. I drew her – how I longed to draw better! – under Rodin's approving eye; but his eye was shrewd as well as approving. For when I asked the lovely creature – what could I do less? – to dine that evening, she promised to come, but I waited in vain; the next day I found that Rodin knew all about it. 'She shall sit for you, *mon ami*, as often as you please, but no dining! I have lost too many models that way!'

Rodin was always drawing; he would walk restlessly round the model, making loose outline drawings in pencil, sometimes adding a light coloured wash. And how he praised her forms! caressing them with his eyes, and sometimes, too, with his hand, and drawing my attention to their beauties. I cared greatly for some early drawings which Rodin showed me at Meudon. These were very powerful, classical and romantic at the same time, evoking sculpture which no one, not even Rodin himself, had attempted. They were magnificent drawings, and I was enthusiastic about them, to Rodin's surprise – and pleasure, I think. No one, he said, had thought much of these scraps – certainly not enough to acquire them. I assured him that English collectors would jump at the chance, and he confided the drawings to my care.

William Rothenstein
Men and Memories, vol. 1, 1934

"Plaster casts of almost everything. The products of an entire century, you might say, an army of work."

Art and technique

Before it can become a plaster, marble or bronze figure, the work modelled by the sculptor must first pass from his hands to those of a whole sequence of craftsmen: casters, enlargers, pointers, assistants, founders and patinaters.

"He had made an Oriental of me, a Tamberlaine, a Genghis Khan", a disappointed Georges Clemenceau said of his bust. Yet the determined, enigmatic character of 'The Tiger' is revealed in the modelling.

Profiles

Rodin succeeded in translating the true appearance of the human body through the accuracy of his multiple profile views.

When I begin a figure, I first study the front, the back and the right and left profiles, that is, the profile views from each of the four directions. Then, with the clay, I establish the overall mass just as I see it and as accurately as possible. Then I work on the intermediary views, which gives me the three-quarter profiles. Then, moving round and round both my clay model and the subject, I compare and refine them....

In a human body the profile is created at the point where the body ends; it is therefore the body that makes the profile. I place my model in such a way that the light, standing out against the background, illuminates the profile. I execute it, I rotate the turntable and that of my model, so that I see a new profile; I turn again, and in this way I gradually work my way around the whole body.

I start again. I tighten up the profiles more and more; and I refine them. As the human body has an infinite number of profiles, I continue introducing new ones as long as I can, or as often as I feel is necessary. As I rotate the turntable, the parts that were in shadow present themselves to the light in their turn; I can therefore see clearly the new profile that I have obtained, for I always work in the light, or at least, as much as possible....

When my profiles are all well defined, they may, with luck, be accurate, but I can only be sure of this when they are checked one against the other, and all together....

It is important to study the profiles from above and below, from high up and low down ... in other words, to gain a good understanding of the solidity of the

Rodin modelling his bust of Falguière, using his profile method. To show the *Balzac* affair had not harmed their friendship, the two sculptors made portrait busts of each other.

human body.... Then I look and I compare with my clay model the plan of the pectoral muscles, the shoulder-blades, the buttocks; I study the bulging muscles of the thighs; and below, the way the feet are planted on the ground. While I was working on *The Age of Bronze* I got hold of one of those ladders that painters use for working on large canvases. I climbed up it and made my clay model match the live model as accurately as I could in foreshortening, and I studied my profiles from above.

You might call what I do 'drawing in depth', because by working according to the method I have described, it is impossible to produce anything flat....

The bringing together of correct profiles, united by accurate intermediary views, results in a faithful image....

When, through the precise execution of profile views, you have entered the realm of truth, the expression seems to arise of its own accord, as if in addition to everything else; the work seems to express itself. In any case, human thought is limited by comparison with what nature transmits directly to us and imposes on us. All that is necessary is to follow the model; character results from its unity....

If a figure is not produced according to these principles and this geometry, it will lack truth, and therefore expression; there will always remain a stubborn lack of communication between it and reality; if it is created merely by inspiration, no matter how elevated or sensitive it may be, it will inevitably be weak, because you can only create from nature. It is nature that makes the artist – once he has understood her and translated her – a creator, or rather her sublime copyist.

Rodin
Conversations with Dujardin-Beaumetz
1913

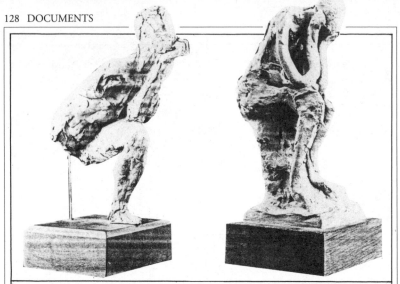

E arly rough sketches for *The Thinker*, modelled in clay. Right: Rodin in front of a plaster cast of the *Victor Hugo* monument, which is being used as a model for the marble version, and (below), a letter to Henri Lebossé, who most frequently did Rodin's casting for him.

Modelling

In the 19th century sculpture was synonymous with modelling in clay. A successful sculptor would never do his own carving; he was surrounded by assistants, or praticiens, *who would carve the marble according to his instructions.*

The *science of modelling* was taught me by one Constant, who worked in the atelier where I made my debut as a sculptor. One day, watching me model a capital ornamented with foliage – 'Rodin,' he said to me, 'you are going about that in the wrong way. All your leaves are seen flat. That is why they do not look real. Make some with the tips pointing towards you, so that, in seeing them, one has the sensation of depth....

'Always remember what I am about to tell you,' went on Constant. 'Henceforth, when you carve, never see the form in length, but always in thickness. Never consider a surface except as the extremity of a volume, as the point, more or less large, which it directs towards you. In that way you will acquire the *science of modelling*.'

This principle was astonishingly fruitful to me. I applied it to the execution of figures. Instead of imagining the different parts of a body as surfaces more or less flat, I represented them as projectures of interior volumes. I forced myself to express in each swelling of the torso or of the limbs the efflorescence of a muscle or of a bone which lay deep beneath the skin. And so the truth of my figures, instead of being merely superficial, seems to blossom from within to the outside, like life itself.

Rodin
Art: Conversations Collected by Paul Gsell
1911

Casting

The cast, which had to be created before a sculpture could be produced in bronze, was either made on the same scale as the original clay model, or enlarged or reduced with the aid of a three-dimensional form of pantograph.

When we speak of a cast, we are no longer dealing with an original, but with a duplicate, from which countless copies may be made. These copies, of plaster, terracotta or, today, in resin, are obtained using 'piece moulds', which can be re-used several times over, because they are designed to be dismantled when the cast is removed from the mould, rather than broken up. These copies enable a work to be circulated for commercial or teaching purposes. The 19th century witnessed the creation of major collections of casts, both private and public.

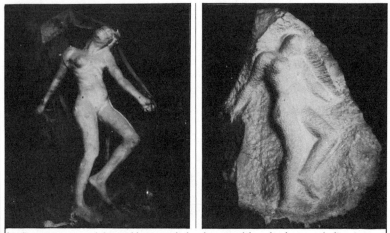

The *praticien* carved the marble to match the plaster model, under the master's directions, using the reference points drilled in the marble block by the pointer to help him.

The process of casting allows the model made of clay or plastilina – materials that are too fragile to last well – to be transformed into a plaster cast, which then becomes the unique, original artwork, both the first clay model and the hollow, reverse mould having been destroyed in the course of the process. After the mould has been made – in one piece in the case of a relief, or in two 'shells' for a sculpture in the round – by applying layers of plaster to the clay model, the latter is removed from inside the mould – and therefore destroyed –– before being replaced by a new material. The destruction, or removal, of the mould is the final stage in the process.

Casting does not take place until the moment when the final model has been executed. It is an indispensable adjunct to the creative process, and, though they may not have gone to the same lengths as Rodin in casting in plaster everything that leaves their hands, in order to preserve it, many sculptors would make clay casts of their first versions, so that they could try out various ideas on the copies without destroying the original, or would experiment with various solutions using plaster copies.

In all these cases, the impression is taken from a clay model. Or it could also be taken directly from nature. The casting of human limbs, drapery and animals was quite acceptable as a working method, but it was understood that such casts should act only as a point of departure. When, as in the case of Roland's *Death of Cato of Utica* in 1783 or Rodin's *Age of Bronze* in the Salon of 1877, the public became convinced that the sculptor had done nothing more than assemble casts taken from life, without any artistic intervention, this could create a scandal highly damaging for an artist at the beginning of his career. Roland and Rodin – who by 1917 did not hesitate to use a cast of his own hand for his

The finished marble carving of *The Martyr* (above). Far left: *The Martyr* in plaster.

Assemblage in Rodin's work

Rodin used figures he had previously created as a sort of image-bank, from which he drew forms to create new works. He was thus the precursor of a technique that has become commonplace in the 20th century.

Everyone is familiar with the group of *The Three Shades* that stands on top of *The Gates of Hell*. Taking the model of his *Adam*, all Rodin did was to modify the treatment of the arms, then assemble three copies of the same figure. We may interpret this as a desire to show the same sculpture at different angles in what was intended to be a frontal composition. Yet we know that these figures were also presented to the public in a different manner, spaced further apart, under the title *The Three Suicides*. This helps us to understand Rodin's main concerns, which are confirmed by the inventory, now in progress, of the casts kept in his property at Meudon. It reveals how he liked to surround himself with a certain number of casts of the same subject, which constituted for him a form of vocabulary, which he would dip into as he searched for inspiration, truncating, adding new elements, simply modifying the original presentation or integrating it into a new composition. Instead of creating endless modulations on the various views of a single human figure, he preferred to create a model that satisfied him entirely, and to use this model to create other compositions.

On several occasions we see how he has assembled several copies of the same figure, thereby giving birth to another new work. First there are the symmetrical assemblages, where the repetition occurs about a single axis, as in the case of *The Three Shades*, *The Three Faunesses*, or *The Secret*, where the same right hand is used

sculpture *The Hand of God* – did their utmost to prove that the works that had come under attack owed the perfection of their anatomy to the sculptor's skill and knowledge of the human body....

The casting of works – a task entrusted to specialized craftsmen, who were nearly always of Italian origin – was mainly carried out in plaster. For a special edition, however, clay was often preferred, as it allowed the sculptor to achieve a more flattering result. Once it had been removed from the mould, it would be fired (having been first hollowed out to prevent it from cracking in the heat); before firing the artist was able to retouch the work and give it once more the vigorous surface texture that cannot be obtained through casting.

Antoinette Le Normand-Romain
Nineteenth-century French Sculpture
Catalogue of an exhibition at the
Grand Palais, Paris, 1986

twice. Then there are the assemblages in which the figures are placed in different planes. This is the case in the *Assemblage of Two Figures of the Night*, a subject one can find in the project for the *Tower of Labour*, or *The Damned*, in which the repetition is intended to be a little more difficult to see. Finally, there are the more elaborate assemblages, with a complex build-up of figures.

Nicole Barbier
Nineteenth-century French Sculpture
Catalogue of an exhibition at the
Grand Palais, Paris, 1986

Marcottage

'An operation that consists in putting together a new work of sculpture by re-using, either partially or in their entirety, works already created by the artist.' Rodin practised *marcottage* very frequently and with great skill, almost always using plaster casts to produce his new compositions. Some of these resulted in 'definitive' new works, which were exhibited, cast in bronze and sold. Others rejoined that often incomprehensible multitude that constituted one of the sources of his creative genius: a collection of experiments, conducted with no clear aim in mind, which were sometimes incoherent, but always intensely personal and independent of any desire to create a specific work of art. A note made of some fleeting moment of inspiration, as if scribbled down in the corner of a notebook, in a piece of plaster, the inner sap sustaining the imagination of its public face.

Several sculptural historians have already mentioned this subject in connection with various works: *The Martyr, Meditation, Ugolino, Kneeling Fauness, The Falling Man*. I would like

A new sculpture is created by juxtaposing the head of one of *The Burghers of Calais* and a female torso.

to add, because of its exceptional use in numerous groups, many of which are very well known, *Fatigue* (which reappears in *Youth Triumphant, The Death of Athens, Paolo and Francesca, The Moon and the Earth, Adam and Eve Asleep*). Finally, it is important to remember that Rodin employed *marcottage* just as much in creating new works designed for public display, as for his personal researches, to project into his materials the frenzy of a wild imagination that his own age would not have understood, and which even today can be disconcerting, frequently evading any interpretations.

Alain Beausire
Nineteenth-century French Sculpture
Catalogue of an exhibition at the
Grand Palais, Paris, 1986

Lost wax casting

Although improvements have been introduced, thanks to modern technology, the technique in use today remains essentially the same as that employed by the Greek sculptors of the 5th century BC. The various processes involved, from the taking of an impression to the pouring of the molten bronze and finishing of the final statue, still demand many hours of patient work. The following pages describe the various stages in the casting of the Little Fauness, *a figure derived from* The Gates of Hell.

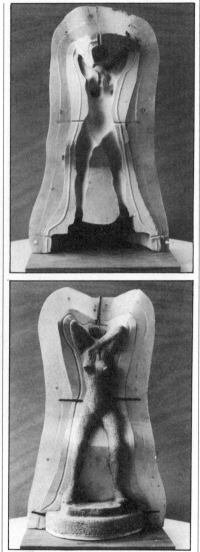

1. The sculptor produces a model, which is generally made of plaster, clay, marble, stone or wood. The surface of the model, the original artwork, is first coated with a substance designed to protect it while the impression is being made.

2. An impression of the model is taken in a bed of a very fine, elastic material, which is supported by a more rigid outer mould. The reinforcing layer is designed to resist the pressure of the molten wax that will later be poured into the mould; for larger works the molten wax is introduced under pressure.

3. The hollow mould is used to create a core of a refractory, or heat-resistant, material, identical to the artist's original model.

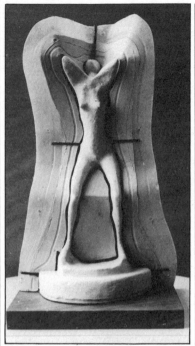

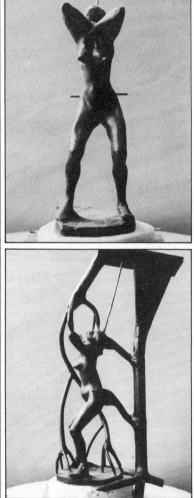

4. The surface of the refractory core is then scraped away. This creates a gap between the core and the mould, into which the wax can be poured. The bronze will eventually be of the same thickness as the space that is created.

5. Once the mould has been closed around the refractory core, the wax is poured into the space that has been introduced between the mould and the core. This stage is essential to obtain a perfect copy of the original sculpture. The mould is then removed, and the resulting wax-covered model can be retouched by hand, to make sure that it matches the original in every detail.

At this point the artist, if he or she wishes, can intervene to retouch the wax model, to make corrections or reinforce a particular effect. This is also the stage at which the artist's signature, the number of the edition and the founder's mark are engraved.

6. A network of wax channels is attached to the wax model. These channels allow the wax to drain away as it is heated and melts; they also help to distribute the molten metal more evenly throughout the mould and allow any gases to escape as the metal is poured in.

7. A fine-grained refractory material is gradually applied to the surface of the wax model and its channels, until the whole thing, supported by a framework, is solid and rigid. The final result, known as the 'casting mould', is then dried and heated. The liquid wax flows out of the mould, leaving a space between the refractory core and the casting mould, which now consists of the refractory material that has been applied over the wax.

8. The casting mould is heated to a very high temperature (550 to 600° C), then covered with an outer layer of cladding, which must be completely dry before the bronze can be poured in.

9. The molten bronze (1200° C) is now poured into the cavity of the mould, filling the space left by the wax. The mould is finally broken open to reveal the metal statue within. The bronze sculpture and its channels are an exact replica of the wax-covered figure (see 6.).

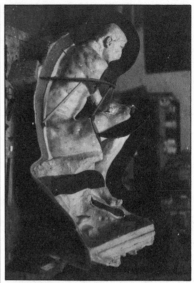

10. The network of supply channels is now cut away, and the surface of the bronze filed and chiselled to remove all traces of them. It is a painstaking and time-consuming task. This process of finishing by hand to bring the bronze to its final state is known as 'chasing'. The remains of the refractory core, which are still inside the bronze statue, are then carefully removed.

Once the chasing is complete, oxides are applied hot or cold to the surface of the bronze to produce a thin layer of corrosion, the patina. This artificial weathering process, called 'patination', protects the bronze from any damage to which it may be subjected over the years. Patinas vary depending on whether the sculpture is intended for display indoors or destined to be exposed to the elements, and may be brown, black, green or bluish, and more or less dark in tone. Today artists can adjust the tones of the patina to accentuate particular effects.

Prepared in collaboration with the Coubertin foundry for the Cantor Foundation

The Thinker in his mould (above) and (below) *Adam*, prior to bronze-casting.

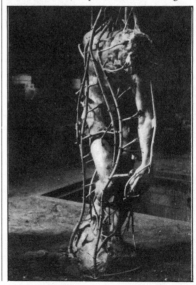

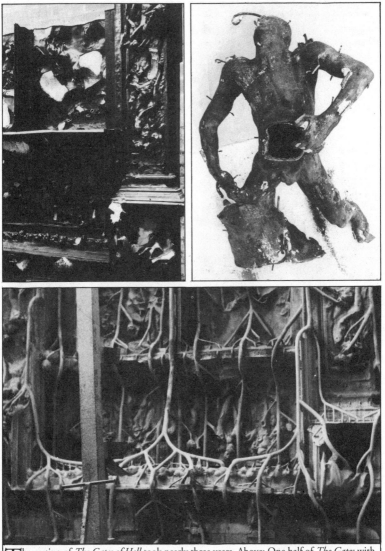

The casting of *The Gates of Hell* took nearly three years. Above: One half of *The Gates* with its network of supply channels for the bronze. Top left: The finished bronze cast of *The Gates* still has gaps, into which figures in the round, cast separately (top right), will be inserted.

FURTHER READING

Beausire, Alain, and Hélène Pinet. *Correspondance de Rodin, 1860–99.* 1985
—, and Florence Cadouot. *Correspondance de Rodin, 1900–7; 1908–2; 1913–7.* 1986–9
Butler, Ruth. *Rodin in Perspective.* 1980
Cassar, Jacques. *Dossier Camille Claudel.* 1987
Champigneulle, Bernard. *Rodin.* 1967
Cladel, Judith. *Rodin: The Man and his Art, with Leaves from his Notebook.* Trans. S. Star. 1914
Elsen, Albert. *'The Gates of Hell' by Auguste Rodin.* 1960
—. *In Rodin's Studio.* 1980
—. *Auguste Rodin: Readings on His Life and Work.* 1965
—. *Rodin's 'Thinker' and the Dilemmas of Modern Public Sculpture.* 1985
—, and Kirk Varnedoe. *The Drawings of Rodin.* 1971
Grappe, Georges. *Catalogue du Musée Rodin.* 1944
Grünefeld, Frederic V. *Rodin: A Biography.* 1987
Gsell, Paul. *Auguste Rodin. Art. Conversations with Paul Gsell.* Trans. Jacques de Caso and Patricia B. Sanders. 1984
Guse, Ernest-Gerhard. *Rodin: Drawings and Watercolours.* 1985
Janson, H. W. *Nineteenth-century Sculpture.* 1985
Judrin, Claudie. *Rodin et les écrivains de son temps.* 1976
— (ed.). *Inventaire des dessins de Rodin.* 4 vols. 1983–9
Laurent, Monique. *Rodin.* 1988
—, and Dominique Vieville. *Auguste Rodin: Le Monument des Bourgeois de Calais.* 1977
Paris, Reine-Marie. *Camille Claudel.* 1984
Pinet, Hélène. *Rodin, sculpteur, et les photographes de son temps.* 1985
Rilke, Rainer Maria. *Rodin.* Trans. Robert Firmage. 1982
Rivière, Anne. *L'Interdite, Camille Claudel.* 1983

EXHIBITION CATALOGUES

The Drawings of Rodin. National Gallery of Art, Washington, D.C., and New York. 1971–2
Lampert, Catherine. *Rodin: Sculpture and Drawings.* Arts Council of Great Britain, London. 1986
Rodin Rediscovered. National Gallery of Art, Washington, D. C. 1981
The Romantics to Rodin: French 19th-century Sculpture from North American Collections. Los Angeles County Museum of Art. 1980

LIST OF ILLUSTRATIONS

All works are by Auguste Rodin, unless otherwise stated.

The following abbreviations have been used: *a* above; *b* below; *c* centre; *l* left; *r* right; Bibl. Nat. Bibliothèque Nationale; Phot. cat. photographic catalogue, Musée Rodin, Meudon; Cat. no. catalogue number, Musée Rodin, Meudon.

Between 1854 and 1857. Charcoal on watermarked cream paper. Cat. no. D5104. *Ibid.*

15*a* Couple after the antique. Between 1854 and 1857. Pencil, pen and brown ink on watermarked cream paper. Cat. no. D5103. *Ibid.*

15*b* Rodin's pass to the imperial museums. *Ibid.*

16 Henri Gervex (1852–1929). *The Painting Jury.* Musée d'Orsay, Paris

17*a* *Self-portrait Wearing a Cap.* Pre-1859. Pencil on cream paper. Cat. no. D119. Musée Rodin, Paris

17*b* Bust of Jean-Baptiste Rodin. 1859. Bronze. Phot. cat. 2310. *Ibid.*

18*al* Rodin and Léon Fourquet. 1862. Photo Braun. Phot. cat. 163. *Ibid.*

18*ar* The demolition of buildings in Paris to create the Rue de Rennes. Engraving from *L'Illustration.* 1868. Bibliothèque des Arts Décoratifs, Paris

18–9 Letter from Jean-Baptiste Rodin to his son. Musée Rodin, Paris

20*l* Rodin with his sister Maria. *c.* 1859. Phot. cat. 2. *Ibid.*

20–1 Rodin with his bust of *The Blessed Father Pierre-Julien Eymard.* 1863. Photo Braun. Phot. cat. 160. *Ibid.*

CHAPTER 2

22 Rodin in 1864. Photo Charles Aubry. Phot. cat. 3. *Ibid.*

23 *Vase des Titans. c.* 1878. Sculpture signed by Carrier-Belleuse, but executed by Rodin. *Ibid.*

24 *Young Woman in a Flowered Hat.* 1865. Terracotta. *Ibid.*

25*al* Honoré Daumier. Drawing of Carrier-Belleuse. Musée du Petit Palais, Paris

25*ar* Portrait of Antoine-Louis Barye. Photo

25*bl* *Mignon.* 1869. Plaster. Musée Rodin, Paris

26 *The Man with the Broken Nose.* 1864. Plaster. Photo Eugène Druet. Phot. cat. 2299. *Ibid.*

27*a* *The Man with the Broken Nose.* 1864. Marble. *Ibid.*

27*b* Old Stock Exchange, Brussels. Photo

28–9 Sheet of sketches made in Italy. *c.* 1875–8. Pencil, pen and brown ink. Cat. D274–9. Musée Rodin, Paris

30 Auguste Neyt, model for *The Age of Bronze.* 1877. Photo Marconi. Phot. cat. 270. *Ibid.*

31*l* *The Age of Bronze.* 1876. Plaster. Photo Marconi. Phot. cat. 269. *Ibid.*

31*r* *The Age of Bronze.* 1877. Bronze. Musée d'Orsay, Paris

32*l* *St John the Baptist.* 1878. Bronze. *Ibid.*

32*r* César Pignatelli, model for *St John the Baptist* and *The Walking Man.* Ecole Nationale Supérieure des Beaux-Arts, Paris

33*a* Torso of *The Walking Man.* 1877. Plaster. Phot. cat. 2193. Musée Rodin, Paris

33*b* *The Walking Man.* 1877. Bronze. Musée d'Orsay, Paris

CHAPTER 3

34 Rodin in his studio with *Adam* and *Eternal Springtime.* 1887. Jessie Lipscomb collection

35 Rodin's studio at Meudon. Phot. cat. 256. Musée Rodin, Paris

36 Study for *The Gates of Hell. c.* 1880. Drawing with brown ink wash. Cat. no. D1963. *Ibid.*

37*a* *Mask of Minos. c.* 1880. Drawing. Cat. no. D1933. *Ibid.*

37*b* Clay sketch for *The Gates of Hell.* 1880–1. *Ibid.*

38*a* Fernand Paillet. Caricature of Rodin. *c.* 1900

38*b* Embracing couple. Drawing for *The Gates of Hell. c.* 1880. Ny Carlsberg Glyptotek, Copenhagen

39*l* *Ugolino.* Drawing for *The Gates of Hell.* 1883. Cat. no. D7627. Musée Rodin, Paris

39*r* Rodin wearing a velvet jacket stained with plaster. 1880. Phot. cat. 311. *Ibid.*

40 Detail from *The Gates of Hell.* 1880–1917. Bronze. *Ibid.*

41*al* *The Three Shades.* 1881. Bronze. *Ibid.*

41*ac* *The Prodigal Son.* 1889. Bronze. *Ibid.*

41*ar* *The Gates of Hell,* as assembled by Léonce Bénédite. 1917. Plaster. *Ibid.*

41*bl* *The Falling Man.* 1882. Bronze. *Ibid.*

41*br* *Fugit Amor.* Bronze. *Ibid.*

42 *The Thinker.* Plaster. Photo Jacques-Ernest Bulloz. *Ibid.*

43*l* *The Thinker* on *The Gates of Hell.* Bronze. *Ibid.*

43*r* *The Thinker.* Small clay model on the scaffolding for *The Gates* in Rodin's studio. 1881. Phot. cat. 289. *Ibid.*

44*a* *Eve. c.* 1880. Plaster. *Ibid.*

44*b* *Ugolino.* 1882. Plaster. *Ibid.*

45*l* *Adam.* Bronze. *Ibid.*

45*r* *She who was Once the Helmet-maker's Beautiful Wife.* 1885. Bronze. *Ibid.*

46 Busts of (1) Antonin Proust. Plaster. Phot. cat. 1428 (2) Roger Marx. Plaster. Phot. cat. 234 (3) Jean-Paul Laurens. Bronze (4) Jules Dalou. Plaster. Phot. cat. 2272. *Ibid.*

47 Busts of (1) Octave Mirbeau. Plaster. Phot.

Phot. cat. 67. *Ibid.*
128 *The Thinker.* First rough clay sketches. *Ibid.*
129*a* Rodin in his studio with the monument to *Victor Hugo.* 1898. Phot. cat. 179. *Ibid.*
129*b* Letter to Henri Lebossé. *Ibid.*
130*l* *The Martyr.* 1885. Plaster. Phot. cat. 306. *Ibid.*
130*r* *The Martyr. c.* 1910. Rough sketch in marble. Phot. cat. 307. *Ibid.*
131 *The Martyr,* or *The Broken Lily.* 1911. Marble. Photo Druet. Phot. cat. 308. *Ibid.*
132 The head of *Pierre de Wissant* juxtaposed

with the *Torso of a Young Woman.* Cat. no. S404. *Ibid.*
133–6*al* Stages in the bronze-casting of the *Little Fauness* at the Coubertin foundry
136*ar* *The Thinker* in its mould, before casting. Coubertin foundry
136*br* *Adam* with its network of channels. *Ibid.*
137*al* Partial casting of *The Gates of Hell. Ibid.*
137*ar* Figure from *The Gates of Hell. Ibid.*
137*b* *The Gates of Hell* with the network of channels. *Ibid.*

INDEX

Figures in italic refer to pages on which captions appear.

PHOTO CREDITS

All rights reserved 25*ar*, 38*a*, 41*br*, 49*ar*, 65, 80, 81*b*, 110. Artephot-Ziollo/Photo Rolland front cover, 23, 25*bl*, 27*b*, 37*b*, 41*al*, 41*ac*, 41*bl*, 45*l*, 45*r*, 47(3), 47(4), 49*b*, 51, 52, 53, 54, 55, 56–7, 58*l*, 59*r*, 60*b*, 60–1, 61*r*, 69*c*, 72, 82*a*, 83*cr*, 86*a*, 87, 90, 104*r*, 108, 110. Artephot-Ziollo 66*b*. © D. Boudinet 24, 40, 43*l*, 73, 97. Bulloz 25*al*, 41*ar*, 42, 44*a*, 46(3). Caisse Nationale des Monuments Historiques et des Sites 92–3*b*. J.-L. Charmet 18*ar*. Coubertin foundation information service/Photo J. Bernard and Y. Bernard 61*c*, 136*ar*, 136*br*, 137*al*, 137*ar*; Photo Y. Bernard 133*l*, 133*ar*, 133*br*, 134*l*, 134*ar*, 134*br*, 135*l*, 135*ar*, 135*br*, 136*al*, 137*b*. Ecole Nationale des Beaux-Arts 32*r*. Giraudon 66*a*. Jessie Lipscomb collection 34, 62. Metropolitan Museum of Art, New York 78. Musée des Beaux-Arts, Poitiers 106. Musée du Petit Palais, Paris 86*b*. © Musée Rodin and © B. Jarret through ADAGP, Paris, 1988 1, 2–3, 4, 5, 6, 7, 14*bl*, 14*br*, 15*a*, 17*a*, 36, 37*a*, 39*l*, 48–9, 69, 88–9, 90. Musée Rodin/B. Jarret spine, back cover, 9, 11, 12*a*, 13, 17*b*, 18*al*, 20*l*, 20–1, 22, 26, 30, 31*l*, 33*a*, 35, 39*r*, 43*r*, 46(1–2), 47(2–3), 47*b*, 48*bl*, 48*br*, 50*b*, 57*ar*, 58–9, 60*al*, 63*l*, 63*r*, 64, 67, 68*a*, 68*b*, 69, 70*b*, 71, 74*ar*, 74*b*, 76*a*, 76*b*, 77, 79, 81*r*, 82*b*, 83*al*, 84*a*, 84*b*, 85*l*, 85*c*, 85*r*, 91, 92, 93*a*, 94–5, 96, 98, 99, 100, 101, 102, 103, 104*l*, 105, 107, 109, 112, 113, 114, 115*al*, 115*ar*, 115*b*, 116, 118*ar*, 119*l*, 119*r*, 120, 121, 122*a*, 125*a*, 125*b*, 126, 127, 128, 129*a*, 130*l*, 130*r*, 131, 132. Musée Rodin/Photo J.-C. Marlaud 12*b*, 15*b*, 18–9, 46(4), 47(1), 122*b*. Musée Rodin/Photo H. Moulonguet 28–9. Ny Carlsberg Glyptotek, Copenhagen 38*b*. Private collections 50*a*, 74*al*, 83*bl*. RMN 10, 14*a*, 16, 31*r*, 32*l*, 33*b*. Roger-Viollet 44*b* (Photo RMN, Vezzavona, Viollet), 70*a*, 75, 111, 112, 129*b* (Harlingue-Viollet). Sirot-Angel 27*b*.

ACKNOWLEDGMENTS

The publishers thank the following for their help: Arsène Bonnafous-Murat, Ruth Butler, RMN publications, Musée Rodin publications, Du Seuil publications, SERS publications, Robert Elborne, the Coubertin foundation, Monique Lepelley-Fonteny, François de Massary, Catherine Mathon, Reine-Marie Paris, and Mrs Joan Vita-Miller of the Cantor collection.

Hélène Pinet
has been curator of the photographic department
at the Musée Rodin in Paris since 1976.
She has written several works,
including *Les Photographes de Rodin*,
published by the Musée Rodin,
and *Rodin, sculpteur, et les photographes de son temps*,
which appeared in 1985.

For Mélanie and Antoine

© Gallimard 1988
English translation © Thames and Hudson Ltd, London,
and Harry N. Abrams Inc., New York, 1992

Translated by Caroline Palmer

Printed and bound in Italy
by Editoriale Libraria, Trieste